DEPRESSION
Light at the End of the Tunnel

JOAN ZAWATZKY

Disclaimer
The characters in this book are fictional and do not refer to real people living or dead. Every effort has been made to make this book as complete and as accurate as possible. This text should be used only as a general guide and not as the ultimate source of information. The ideas, suggestions and strategies described in this book are intended to provide helpful information and are not a replacement for the care and supervision of a qualified health professional. All problems and concerns regarding your health require the supervision of a qualified medical doctor. If you have any pre-existing medical disorders consult your doctor before following any of the suggestions, techniques or strategies in this book. The author and publisher are not responsible for any negative consequences that result from reading this book.

Please note
In this book the masculine pronoun "he" is generally used when referring to the client or therapist. This is for convenience and does not reflect a preference for either sex.

Revised edition: Veritax 2013
Melbourne Victoria Australia, 2013
www.placeofbooks.com

First published by Hybrid Publishers, 2002
There's a Light at the End of the Tunnel
Melbourne, Victoria, Australia.

Typeset and cover design by BookPOD
Cover image iStockphoto

ISBN: 978-0-9873302-3-9 (pbk)
eISBN: 978-0-9873302-4-6 (ebook)

A Catalogue-in-Publication is available from the National Library of Australia.

For all those battling to overcome depression.

A NOTE FROM THE AUTHOR

A revised edition

Since writing my first book on depression, *There's a Light at the End of the Tunnel* in 2002, the desperation I have seen in depressed people is even more pronounced. Doctors are writing more prescriptions for antidepressants and there is talk of a depression epidemic.

I have revised this book and added to its content to respond to these needs by including practical new strategies and information about up to date techniques to overcome depression. More healing stories and case histories have been added to inspire your fight to overcome depression.

There is no such thing as one approach suited for each person or that each person should be limited to only one approach. This book provides you with several of the most successful ways of treating depression, so that if one method doesn't suit you or help to beat your depression, another will. My hope is that you will find relief from your depression, as you work through this special mix of healing tales and strategies.

A resource for family friends and caregivers

With the increase of teenagers and even children suffering from depression, I have added chapters providing you with guidelines to help you with issues such as bullying at school, cyber bullying, drug and alcohol abuse, self-harm and suicide. Caring for an aged parent and the difficulties involved with living with a depressed partner have also been included.

This book will provide you with a solid understanding of the causes and symptoms of depression, strategies to fight it and the practical and emotional support necessary to help your depressed loved ones.

Contents

PART 1: UNDERSTANDING THE BASICS

PART 2: THE INNER ROUTE

PART 3: THE CONSTRUCTIVE ROUTE TO THINKING, FEELING AND ACTING

.

PART 5: HARMONY AND BALANCE

PART 6: TREATMENT FOR DEPRESSION

PART 7: DEPRESSION IN SPECIAL GROUPS – CHILDREN, TEENAGERS, THE AGED, A LOVED ONE

PART 8: SUICIDE

INTRODUCTION

Most of us feel sad or miserable from time to time but if a down mood has not lifted for several weeks, then you might be experiencing depression. Assess your mood by answering the following questions:

- Are you finding your life more difficult to manage?

- Have you tried to improve your life but hit a brick wall?

- Has the pleasure gone from things you once enjoyed?

- Do you struggle to concentrate and find you are becoming forgetful?

- Are you having trouble sleeping though you feel tired a lot of the time?

- Do you feel a failure and the future seems to hold no hope?

- Have you withdrawn from your friends and social activities?

- Have you lost your appetite or are you eating more than usual?

If the answer is "yes" to all or most of these questions, you may be depressed, and it's time to do something about it. You are not alone. More people are depressed and struggling to cope than ever. Depression is a serious condition that appears in many different forms and affects each of us differently, but it is highly treatable. Not only can you help yourself by following the recommendations in this book but there is information about medical and natural therapies to turn to for assistance.

To encourage your recovery, this book provides you with the following powerful blend of practical strategies:

1. *Cognitive behavioural therapy (CBT)* is a highly regarded and fast-acting technique used world-wide to improve a depressed mood by changing the way you think and feel about yourself, others and life in general. By using CBT you will learn to become more positive,

gain self-esteem and develop new and constructive ways of handling situations.

2. *Mindfulness-based cognitive therapy (MBCT)* uses some of the skills learned from CBT and combines them with a technique that focuses on awareness of the present moment and viewing life in an objective way. It especially targets the prevention of recurrences of depression.

3. *Case histories* about sufferers from various types of depression and their ways of overcoming it, are included throughout the book to make the information about depression more real and understandable.

4. *Healing stories* found after most chapters will provide you with an additional and inspirational approach to assist you in finding helpful answers and making positive changes.

5. *Medical and natural treatments for depression.* Years ago traditional medicine and alternative therapies rarely appeared at the same time, but in this book you'll find them working together holistically to help you.

This book offers self-help for sufferers of various types of depression, but if you feel that your world is collapsing around you or you have thoughts of suicide, self-help is *not* the path to follow at this time. Seek immediate professional help from your doctor, hospital, psychiatrist, psychologist or social worker.

PART 1

UNDERSTANDING THE BASICS

ONE

UNDERSTANDING DEPRESSION

Sadness and depression are often confused

Depression and sadness are often confused. It is "normal" to be upset or even miserable about a life event that turns out badly, to feel discouraged or to grieve for a loved one. However, when the sadness lingers for long periods and feelings of despair rob the quality of your life, you are depressed. The intense pain of depression not only affects you, but your family and close friends as well. Depression is a real and debilitating disorder that is not due to a weak personality, flaws in your character or lack of willpower.

Depression can strike at any time and people of any age, sex or race can suffer from it. According to the World Health Organisation 350 million people are suffering from depression and it will become "the leading cause of the global burden of disease by 2030". Depression does not have a single cause or show itself in exactly the same way in each person and it can exist independently or together with other illnesses.

The signs of depression

The most common signs of depression are found in the following areas of functioning:

Thinking

Depression promotes negative thoughts and causes you to focus on your guilt, inadequacies, failures and fears. Repetitive, nagging thoughts may make you question your actions and motives, and criticise yourself for your failures. Your most dangerous thoughts may be of ending your anguish through suicide.

Emotions

You feel sad and despairing and cry frequently or complain of being numb and empty. Nothing seems pleasurable, and the feelings of love or affection you once had for those close to you seems to have disappeared. Vulnerable and confused, you are afraid of people and things that were not frightening before. The future looks bleak and overwhelming.

Energy and motivation

Some days you feel so tired that you have difficulty dragging yourself out of bed. Even the smallest task takes on daunting proportions as your energy deserts you. You have lost interest in doing things you once enjoyed and nothing seems worth the struggle.

Movement

Your body and mind feel as if they are in slow motion and you are unable to complete activities that once took you a short time. Some people feel restless and agitated, moving around aimlessly, or attempting several tasks without finishing any of them.

Concentration and memory

Concentrating on reading, writing a letter or watching television is a thing of the past. Performing intricate tasks such as sewing, home repairs or following a conversation, is difficult. Your formerly sharp memory may have deteriorated to such an extent that sometimes you can't remember what you did yesterday. Some people are so impaired that they fear the onset of dementia.

Images

When depressed you may describe the way you feel in terms of darkness, or being stuck. You might talk of being trapped or "the return of the black dog".

Physical changes

Depression interferes with your sleeping and eating patterns and you might notice that your sex drive is lower. Poor appetite and weight loss is another characteristic though occasionally depressed people sleep and eat excessively. Muscular aches and pains, headaches and gastro-intestinal problems may bother you. You even look tired and worn out, as if you are carrying the troubles of the world on your shoulders.

> Depression can differ in type and intensity and strike in a variety of ways. Though each person experiences depression differently, there are some common signs. The stronger the symptoms are and the longer they have bothered you, the more attention you need to give them.

Use of labels

The use of labels and the categorising of symptoms of depression is a clinical approach to the condition, used mainly by professionals working in the field. However, it can be helpful and of value to identify the different types of depression.

TYPES OF DEPRESSION

Major (Severe) depression

Of all types of depression, major depression is the most intense and disabling. It is characterised by despair and hopelessness so devastating that suicide can be a danger. Major depression can occur suddenly or develop over many months. It may begin at any age, but the average age of onset is the mid-twenties.

Major depression is the most debilitating form of depression. Its despair and hopelessness is so profound that nothing seems of interest or gives you pleasure. Sometimes your fatigue is so overwhelming that you find it impossible to get out of bed. You have no appetite and may hardly sleep for days. You may experience brooding, negative, guilt-laden thoughts, concerns about your health and feelings of panic. Numbness or hollowness and lack of belonging are common symptoms so devastating, that suicide is a danger.

Symptoms

To diagnose major depression, psychiatrists will expect the following symptoms to have been present for at least a period of two weeks.

- Constant depressed mood.
- Insomnia.
- Marked loss of interest and pleasure in life.
- Fatigue and energy loss.
- Recurrent thoughts of death and suicide.
- Indecisiveness.
- Feelings of worthlessness and guilt.
- Inability to concentrate.
- Restless agitation or feeling extremely slowed down.

Case study

Ken sat tensely, jaw set and eyes glaring. His clothes were crumpled, his face gaunt, eyes lacklustre and his hair a scruffy mess. He looked older than his twenty-three years. Three months earlier he had attempted suicide with an overdose of sleeping tablets but fortunately friends found him in time and he was rushed to hospital, where psychiatrists diagnosed major depression. After spending two months in hospital, his depression was no longer as severe but he continued to have periods of deep gloom.

When Ken visited his general practitioner, Dr Wilson, he refused to return to the city hospital out-patient department. When Dr Wilson suggested he see a local counsellor, he reluctantly agreed. Dr Wilson referred Ken to me.

"I must have had a weak moment when I agreed to see you today. I didn't want to see a counsellor. If you can't help me no one can," he said glumly.

I tried to reassure him but he looked away, speaking slowly, as he stared listlessly at the carpet. "I can't see a way out of this. I don't enjoy anything anymore and I must be lousy company. Even my girlfriend has left me, but who'd blame her, living with such a loser."

He told me how he had battled to cope with his work as a computer programmer. He had become slow and had lost confidence in making the tough decisions. "Worst of all, I couldn't keep my mind on track and I mucked up an important programme a few days before I cracked up." He shook his head and kept his eyes averted.

"When you say you cracked up...what happened?" I asked.

He explained that he was sitting at his desk with his head in his hands. "I sobbed really loudly. The whole office heard me and came running." He smiled cynically. "They stood around my desk, not knowing what to do. Anyway they packed up my stuff and one of the guys drove me home."

He told me how his mother called the doctor and that he was sent to hospital where he saw a psychiatrist who put him on tablets. He hadn't worked since.

"I think of dying a lot these days.... but don't worry I won't try suicide though I'd probably be better off dead."

Depression ran in Ken's family. His grandmother, a first cousin and his sister are all depressives and his brother Eric attempted suicide three years ago.

"I've been running away from the blues all my life and now it's catching up with me. It all seems too hard...I don't know how I'm going to make it through the rest of my life."

Mild depression (dysthymia)

Dysthymia is sometimes referred to as mild depression and is less severe than major depression. Diagnosis of dysthymia is often difficult because of the subtle nature of the symptoms. Sufferers might manage to function marginally for about two years and sometimes longer before the depression is diagnosed. They might even believe that depression is a part of their character and not discuss their symptoms with doctors, family members, or friends. Diagnosis of dysthymia can be difficult if it occurs at the same time as other psychological disorders, which adds a level of complexity in determining its presence. If left untreated it may develop into severe depression.

Case study

Karen buried her face in her hands and sobbed. "Justin left me last week. After seven years of marriage, he packed his things and walked out, without a word or thought for me or the kids. I haven't had the courage to tell them yet. They adore their dad, so I don't know what I'll say to them." She wiped away her tears with a crumpled tissue. "I've seen this coming. Things haven't been that good between us. We've hardly said a word to each other lately and I've had a feeling that he was seeing someone else though he denied it."

She needed to talk so I didn't interrupt her.

"About two and a half years ago I started to feel really tired and down... an empty kind of hopelessness. I thought I had a virus, but the doctors couldn't find anything. At work my confidence dried up and I couldn't concentrate. I struggled to decide the simplest things, even like what clothes to wear in the morning. No wonder I lost my job."

She ran her hands through her hair. "Look at me, I'm a total mess. Who could blame him for turning away from me? He's had a lot to put up with." She continued, "Now that he's gone, it's like a movie in my head... my mind goes over and over the hurt."

"Are you managing to sleep?" I asked.

"I don't sleep for more than two hours a night...and I've started smoking again."

"And your appetite?"

"The sight of food makes me feel sick but I'm forcing myself to eat. I've got to keep going for the children."

Endogenous and reactive depression

Endogenous depression occurs without obvious cause and is considered to be mainly of chemical or biological origin and often runs in families. The symptoms of endogenous depression are similar to those of major or severe depression and suicide can be a danger.

Reactive depression occurs when sadness due to disappointment, emotional distress or loss becomes prolonged and intense, as in bereavement, extensive financial loss, the ending of a relationship or a ruined career. Reactive depression can result in hopelessness, anxiety, irritability, anger and a preoccupation with upsetting thoughts, but with time and support these symptoms usually disappear.

These two labels to describe depression are often used for convenience.

A daily mood chart

Recording your mood is an excellent way of monitoring your progress. It is so easy to forget small changes in mood from week to week. Making a mark once or twice a day on a sheet you've printed out, allows you to monitor not only your mood but your hours of sleep, any events that triggered a change in the way you feel and your current medication. You can add in anything relevant that may have affected your mood such as alcohol, illicit drugs, pain or anxiety. This record allows you to monitor your own moods correctly and it also a helpful document to show your doctor or therapist.

Keeping a mood chart until you feel entirely well, allows you to not only to appreciate your progress but to understand many factors like triggers to your depression, how your depression manifested itself and the medications you took and their effect.

How to fill in the mood chart

The top line reflects the days in a two week period (14). Down the left side is a 1 to 10 rating that will denote your mood for the day. If you wish you can add in a second set of ratings to measure your mood twice that day. Once the two week period has been completed you can connect the dots marked on the page and you will have a mood graph.

DAILY MOOD CHART (TWO WEEKS)

Days in two weeks of the month		1	2	3	4	5	6	7	8	9	10	11	12	13	14
GOOD DAY	10														
Rate each day with 10 being a good day and 1 being a poor day.	9														
	8														
	7														
	6														
	5														
	4														
	3														
	2														
POOR DAY	1														
Sleep – number of hours per day.															
Depression triggers															
Medication															
Any other information or positive/ negative events															
Emotions															
Pain															

The line between anxiety and depression

Over recent years, researchers have come to the conclusion that people who are vulnerable to anxiety can be equally vulnerable to depression and that symptoms of anxiety and depression often overlap. Though depression is usually a state of minimal energy and anxiety is an elevated energy state, the two can exist simultaneously.

Anxiety and depression are in essence, very different. Depression makes you feel despairing and you may struggle to cope with your daily life. Anxiety or even fear in the face of danger is a normal reaction that prepares you to fight or to run.

With the "fight or flight response" adrenalin surges through your system. It is accompanied by fast breathing and heart rate increasing the oxygen levels in your bloodstream. Blood shifts to the muscles to enable you to act.

If you're anxious you may feel a constant nagging uncertainty or apprehension. Similar feelings may develop in a state of panic without you being aware of a recognisable trigger. The intense form of anxiety suffered by many people is far greater than the usual range of anxiety or stress we all know; such as the anxiety felt before an exam or when tackling a difficult task. This anxiety is intense and debilitating.

Just imagine being depressed but at the same time, feeling wound up and wringing your hands. You can't concentrate or do anything worthwhile to resolve whatever is worrying you. Feeling powerless to help yourself makes you more anxious. It follows, that your inability to do anything to help yourself also increases your depression.

Fortunately new medications prescribed by doctors can often relieve both symptoms. However, psychological help in addition to medication can usually be of further assistance.

TWO

BIPOLAR DISORDER (MANIC DEPRESSION)

Bipolar disorder occurs in two forms: bipolar 1 and bipolar 2.

Bipolar 1 disorder

This disorder was once known commonly as manic depression. It is a dramatic form of depression, characterised by cyclical extremes in mood. Approximately 1% of the population suffer from it and it affects an equal number of men and women. The first episode of bipolar 1 disorder is likely to occur in the late teens and twenties or later in the forties.

Mania results in exuberant talk that is often fast and incessant. A person in this state may have excessive energy, increased libido, high productivity and grandiose ideas. Then, like a sudden storm, a "high" mood can plummet to an unbearable "low". Now the person lacks interest in everything, thought and action are slowed, and exhaustion is overwhelming.

Manic symptoms usually appear suddenly. Though they may be welcomed after a period of depression, within a few days the early phase of elation, confidence and productivity can give way to unpleasant out-of-control feelings of racing, pressured thoughts that seem to flow faster than the person can speak or write. An uncomfortable restlessness and distractibility may result in movement from one task to another.

Spike Milligan, one of Britain's most popular comic writers and performers, described his manic episodes: "The best scripts I wrote were when I was ill ... A mad desire to be better than anybody else at comedy, and if I couldn't do it in the given time of eight hours a day, I used to work 12, 13 and 14. I was determined. There was a time when I was positively manic. I was four feet above the ground at times, talking twice as fast as normal people ... I was pressured inside. I couldn't sleep, couldn't control it."

In its early stages this disorder may go unnoticed, and even when mood swings develop, family and friends may still not recognise the signs. They may think the person is being difficult and blame the changes in behaviour on outside stresses or drug and alcohol abuse.

Symptoms of a manic phase

If you or someone you know has bipolar disorder, review this list of symptoms typical of the manic phase:

- Inflated, self-confident mood.

- Impaired judgment and grandiose ideas.

- Decreased need for sleep.

- Excessive and unusual talkativeness, with rapid, distracted and disconnected speech.

- Ideas racing and thoughts pounding uncontrollably.

- Increased activity and a tendency to work on several plans at once.

- Restlessness, agitation and irritability.

- Excessive and reckless involvement in pleasurable activities that may lead to dangerous consequences (e.g. sex, alcohol and drug abuse, overspending, gambling, unsound financial decisions).

- At the height of the manic phase, symptoms may become psychotic.

- Behaviour may become antisocial.

Symptoms of a depressive phase

The symptoms of this phase are similar to those of severe depression. Thoughts, emotions, behaviour and feelings are predominantly sad and despairing.

Case study

"I hope this won't take too long," Pamela said as she tapped the floor with her high-heeled shoe. "I have masses to do today and I'm feeling great," she said speaking fast.

Her body was tense and her eyes darted around the room. She was dressed in a figure-hugging, red pantsuit and her chestnut hair cascaded around her shoulders in curls.

"I'm going to enjoy this high," she said exuberantly. "Tonight I plan to go to the disco with my friend and dance, dance, dance till late. I can't get to bed for ages anyhow, I've far too many ideas swirling around. Even now my mind is racing, like a machine turned on high with no medium." She continued. "Anyway, I think I'd best get moving, can't spend my day sitting here any longer, things to do. See you later."

Two weeks later, Pamela sat slumped in the same chair. This time she wore no make-up, her hair was scraped back and she looked pale in her dull outfit. She could almost have been a different person to the excited, expansive Pamela I had seen before.

"I've come down with a real bump. I hate these mood swings – the agony and the ecstasy. If only I was like everyone else I know, predictable and boring." She sighed deeply. "I can't even seem to keep a relationship on track. Did you know that Nicholas left me?"

Weeks later when Pamela's general practitioner decided she needed medication, he referred her to a psychiatrist. After her first appointment with the psychiatrist she was in tears. "He said that I have a bipolar disorder and prescribed Lithium," she said with a sob. "It's really scary knowing that I have a weird illness and will need to take medication for a long time."

When I saw her again two months later, she was neither high nor low. She was dressed modestly, her hair caught at the nape of her neck and she smiled.

"I'm nothing like the Pamela I was before. I'm more steady now, and I can plan to do things...but I do miss the fun of my highs."

Bipolar 2 disorder

Bipolar 2 disorder is similar to bipolar 1, with episodes of depression and elevated moods that do not reach the intensity of mania and are known as *hypomania*. Between the two extreme phases a person feels stable and can function normally.

One of the characteristics of bipolar 2 is *rapid cycling*. Within days or even hours, a person's mood can change from high to low in what is known as a *mixed episode*. The diagnosis of rapid cycling dissorder is made when mood changes occur at least four times within a year.

Bipolar 2 is believed to be under diagnosed because it is often mistaken for normal energetic and action- oriented behaviour. A person experiencing a high or hypomanic phase can be infectious, positive and fun to be with. However, there can be a downside to *hypomania*, as there might be a tendency for a person to spend excessively, seek out sexual partners when they usually would not and engage in all sort of risks.

Causes of bipolar disorder

As yet, researchers have not as yet identified a clear cause for bipolar disorder. There is evidence that genetic predisposition is likely to be involved. Imbalances are indicated in brain chemicals during changing mood cycles. Bipolar depression is also influenced by psychological and social factors, and the stresses of life's events play a significant role in a person's vulnerability to this illness.

The effects of bipolar disorder on a relationship

Living with someone who has bipolar disorder can be extremely trying. A partner's lack of stability and sudden mood changes may be baffling. Irritability and argumentativeness together with sudden spending or gambling sprees are common if a partner suffers from this disorder. Repeated episodes of irresponsible and often irrational behaviour may result in a communication breakdown. Excessive demands for sex is often followed by lack of interest during the depressive phase. To prevent deterioration in a relationship, both partners might benefit from counselling to help them to live with the specific problems of bipolar disorder.

Cyclothymic disorder

This is a milder form of bipolar disorder in which a person has mood swings over a period of years that range from mild depression to emotional highs. Though not as serious as bipolar disorder, cyclothymia can disrupt a life and turn relationships and work situations into a nightmare. As with the other forms of depression, chemical imbalance and genetic factors are suspected.

The characteristics that typify cyclothymic behaviour are impulsiveness and restlessness. People with cyclothymia are often easily bored, talkative, persuasive and quick-witted. The most striking characteristics are instability, which is noticeable in uneven job performance, frequent job changes, and a tendency towards being erratic in private life, resulting in broken relationships.

Case study

It was Joe's first visit to a counsellor. He shuffled his feet and fiddled with the buttons on his shirt. Then, with the ease of a salesman, he ran through all the reasons for not needing to see me.

"Yeah, I'm moody at work some of the time and I've had a few run-ins with customers who act like morons. So, big deal! That doesn't mean I need a shrink or I'm sick."

Joe complained endlessly about his boss. "According to the boss, I've got problems but I can't see it. The other day, he told me that I was a great salesman and that he appreciated me...but that soon I'd go too far with my smart aleck remarks and admiring the ladies." Joe shook his head in disbelief. He insisted that there hadn't been a single complaint from customers. "He told me to get some counselling...or else. But I like the way I am and I'm not changing. At least I get great ideas and I'm not dead inside like some people I know."

I didn't expect to see Joe again.

Mood chart for all bipolar disorders

A daily mood chart

As in unipolar depression, recording changes on a mood chart will help you to be more aware and informed. The information is repeated for your convenience.

Recording your mood is an excellent way of monitoring your progress. It is so easy to forget small changes in mood from week to week. Making a mark once or twice a day on a sheet you've printed out, allows you to monitor not only your mood but your hours of sleep, any events that triggered a change in the way you feel and your current medication. You can add in anything relevant that may have affected your mood such as alcohol, illicit drugs, pain or anxiety. This record allows you to monitor your own moods correctly and it also a helpful document to show your doctor or therapist.

Keeping a mood chart until you feel entirely well, allows you to not only appreciate your progress but to understand many factors like triggers to your depression, how your depression manifests itself and the medications you took and their effect.

How to fill in the mood chart

The top line reflects the days in a two week period (14 days.) Down the left side is a mood rating from "extremely manic" or "high" to "extremely depressed". Note your mood changes for the day.

1. You can mark your mood more than once a day if it changes or "cycles". Mark your first mood with a cross at the appropriate day and level and use another symbol or change in colour for a second or third mood change that day.

2. Write down the name of medications and doses you are taking. This might be altered by your doctor and it is important to look at your mood changes in respect of the medication you are taking.

3. Note how long you slept at night.

4. Record any triggers to a mood change or special events. Women should make a note of monthly hormonal changes.

5. Once the two week period has been completed you can connect the dots marked on the page and you will have a mood graph.

MOOD CHART FOR ALL BIPOLAR DISORDERS
(FOR A PERIOD OF TWO WEEKS)

Days in two weeks of the month	1	2	3	4	5	6	7	8	9	10	11	12	13	14
Rate mood swings each day														
Extremely manic or "high"														
Manic														
Moderately manic														
Mildly manic														
Stable mood														
Mildly depressed														
Moderately depressed														
Severely depressed														
Extremely depressed														
SLEEP AT NIGHT– NUMBER OF HOURS														
DEPRESSION TRIGGERS (For women also note hormonal changes)														
MEDICATION														

Days in two weeks of the month	1	2	3	4	5	6	7	8	9	10	11	12	13	14
ANY OTHER POSITIVE OR NEGATIVE EVENTS OR FEELINGS TO RELATE														
ANXIETY														
PAIN														

The link between creativity and mood disorder

Is there a link between the creative expression of writers, poets, painters and musicians and mood disorders? Artists Georgia O'Keefe and Jackson Pollock, composers Robert Schumann and Hector Berlioz, writers Joseph Conrad, Charles Dickens, Leo Tolstoy, Henry James, William Styron, Herman Melville and Herman Hesse and playwright Eugene O'Neill, were all plagued by depression. Many top actors and actresses admit to having a bipolar condition.

A wide body of research indicates that writers and poets are disproportionately affected by mood disorders and even more so bipolar disorder. The eighteenth and nineteenth century poets Percy Bysshe Shelley, Lord Alfred Tennyson, Lord Byron, John Keats, William Blake, Walt Whitman, Samuel Taylor Coleridge, Edgar Allen Poe and Robert Burns had periods in their lives when they struggled with depression and mood swings. Later poets, Emily Dickinson and Jon Berryman, also suffered from mood disorders, as did popular composers and musicians Cole Porter, Irving Berlin, Charles Mingus and Charlie Parker.

A study of 700,000 adults that was reported in the British Journal of Psychiatry shows that students with former straight-A scores were four times more likely to be bipolar than their peers. Many other studies provide evidence that there may be a link between bipolar disorder and creative genius.

Kay Redfield Jamison, a writer, psychiatrist and herself a sufferer of bipolar disorder, discusses the link between creativity and bipolar disorder in *Touched with Fire:* "Occasionally an exhilarating and powerful creative force, more often a destructive one, manic depressive illness gives a touch of fire to many of those who experience it ... one that confers advantage but often kills and destroys as it does so." When Kay Redfield Jamison studied 47 British writers, painters, and sculptors from the Royal Academy, she discovered that a large number had been treated for bipolar disorder. Half of the poets, who were the largest group suffering from bipolar disorder were being treated with medication.

During a phase of hypomania, flowing and frequent thinking, flair, insight, unusual and interesting perceptions occur. It is a time when creative people tend to break with constraints and believe they are capable of almost anything. Then during the down phase, many do the basic "hack work" of editing and putting their concepts together.

THREE

OTHER FORMS OF DEPRESSION

Adjustment Disorder

Adjustment disorder refers to an abnormal and extreme response to a particularly stressful, identifiable event or change in a person's life. It is often accompanied by tearfulness, sadness and feelings of despair.

Symptoms of adjustment disorder

- Sadness
- Nervousness
- Anxiety
- Depression
- Inability to enjoy things that were once pleasurable
- Feeling overwhelmed and unable to cope
- Trouble sleeping
- Crying spells

Each person reacts differently to stressful events depending on their ability to cope. Certain periods of one's life make one more vulnerable to an adjustment depression. The symptoms are usually milder than other forms of depression and last for a shorter period. Once the stressor has been identified and no longer poses a problem, recovery from this disorder usually takes up to six months. Some people tend to have symptoms for longer. If symptoms continue, a more severe depression may be diagnosed and professional help will be necessary.

Typical stressors that trigger adjustment disorder

- The death of a loved one.
- The loss of a job or retirement.
- Divorce or relationship problems.
- Flood, fire or other catastrophes.
- Moving house, moving to a different city or country.
- Physical assault.
- Worries about money.
- Serious illness in yourself or a loved one.

It is important to distinguish between this form of depression and a post-traumatic stress disorder, which is an overwhelming persistent reaction towards an event that threatens the life or safety of a person.

Adjustment disorders are common among young people without the maturity or experience to back them or the elderly, who may become excessively upset about circumstances or events that increase their sense of helplessness and vulnerability.

Adjustment disorders typically manifest themselves in an inability to function at work, studies and in social activities and relationships. They also may take the form of an extreme or excessive reaction to the event or situation that initiated the stress. Symptoms vary in individuals but may include the following:

Triggers of stress in teenagers and young adults

- Family problems or conflict.
- Inability to cope with the academic demands at school.
- Peer pressures.

- Bullying.
- Sexuality issues.

Case study

Marie was blue eyed and twenty-one. Hurt was etched on her attractive face. She fingered the small diamond ring on the third finger of her left hand, all she had left of Danny. One minute they were booking the reception hall for their wedding and the next he told her that he didn't want to marry her or be tied down. He kissed her cheek and left. She hadn't seen him for months.

"I don't understand what I've done wrong, why he doesn't love me. I'm crazy about him. It's got to be my fault. If I hadn't hassled him about the fancy, big reception then maybe he'd still be here. I'm so hurt inside. I'll never, ever get over it."

Marie hadn't eaten for days and was sleeping badly.

"My mind is such a mess that I can't work or think of anything else but Danny. I can't imagine living without him."

Marie struggled to cope with work and refused all social invitations for months. A work friend talked her into joining a netball team, and that made all the difference. She met a new group of people and with their support she gradually began to go out again.

Atypical depression

The main characteristics of atypical depression, distinguishing it from other forms of depression, are what psychiatrists call "mood reactivity". The mood of a person who is severely depressed might improve suddenly if something positive is experienced. In major depression, positive changes will not bring on a change in mood. Atypical depression is usually characterized by the following signs:

- Sleeping too much.
- Increased appetite or weight gain.

- An intense reaction or increased sensitivity to rejection, resulting in problems with relationships.
- Having a feeling of being weighed down or leaden.

Substance-induced depression

Substance-induced disorders should be seen as distinct from independently occurring disorders like depression. However, substance-induced disorders may occur simultaneously with existing underlying emotional illnesses. A wide range of substances, including prescription drugs, illicit drugs and alcohol, can create or worsen depression. Symptoms can range from mild anxiety to severe depression, full blown mania and psychosis. Most substance-induced symptoms improve once the person stops taking the substance. However, use of some substances is known to trigger depression and other mental illnesses. If addiction occurs the depression may continue indefinitely

Substances that can affect mood

- Alcohol
- Caffeine
- Cocaine and amphetamines
- Hallucinogens
- Nicotine
- Opioids
- Sedatives

Some prescription medications for controlling blood pressure and cardiac problems, a number of antihistamines, benzodiazepines, and anti-cancer drugs can cause depression.

Treatment

Psychiatric treatment and counselling is an important part of therapy for a person who has a substance-induced depression. Due to the period of withdrawal with its intense craving for the substance and unpleasant reactions such as tremors, rapid heart rate, agitation and hallucinations, supervision, possibly in a hospital or a detoxification centre is recommended. Later attending support groups is an important part of therapy. In the long term, recovery will depend to a large extent on the person's avoidance of people who encourage addiction and the person's awareness of the stresses that act as triggers.

Case study

Grant rubbed his bloodshot eyes and looked at me sheepishly. "I've gone and done it again. You'd have thought I'd learn from my mistakes. It felt like a huge dark hole inside me so I started on the beer. I don't know how many I had and can't remember what happened after that. I woke at about midday with a pounding head and sick feeling. Worst of all, I felt really low so I drink to get rid of that feeling...but after drinking it hits me twice as hard."

Grant had struggled on for about a year until he made up his mind to seek counselling. He had been divorced a few years earlier and hadn't come to terms with the split. He felt resentful that his wife had left him for a younger man. He was still drinking, but far less. During his sessions he came to terms with his hurt.

It was then that he decided to quit drinking. As he had already cut down it was much easier than he had hoped. Perhaps it was the voluntary work he was doing with children that helped to involve him and take his mind off his own troubles. He did go through a tough period of withdrawal from the alcohol but he managed to cope. He says he still longs for a beer when he's with his mates but he hasn't given in yet.

Novelist William Styron, in his book, *Darkness Visible*, recounts how alcohol, once his friend, betrayed him: "It struck me quite suddenly, almost overnight: I could no longer drink. It was as if my body had risen up in protest, along with my mind, and had conspired to reject this daily moodbath which it had so long welcomed and who knows, perhaps even come to need."

🔑 Substance abuse and its relationship to depression and other mood disorders is a topic so immense that detail about it is beyond the scope of this book. There is a great deal of information available on the Internet and in books and journals written specifically about this subject.

FOUR

PHYSIOLOGICAL CAUSES OF DEPRESSION

You might have asked yourself many times where this illness that drains your energy and your joy of life comes from, or why it makes you feel a despair that tears you apart. There is no single answer. Depression is a complex condition. It can strike suddenly and its duration can be brief or lengthy, with no obvious reason. Researchers believe that depressed moods usually result from a combination of hereditary, psychological, biological and environmental factors. Understanding more about the causes of depression will provide you with invaluable information about factors that spark your own depression.

There are several physiological factors that may contribute to a person's susceptibility to depression. This chapter discusses the most common factors.

Hereditary causes

Depression is an illness that can run in families. If you look into your family background you might find parents, grandparents or siblings, who are or have been depressed. If your parents suffer from depression, then you are more likely to develop that condition than a person whose parents are not depressed. Though genes can influence the development of depression or predispose you to it, genetic inheritance doesn't necessarily mean that you will develop it. If your upbringing was stable and you have learned sound coping mechanisms for stress you may go through life untouched by depression.

Studies of identical twins have revealed interesting results due to shared genetic inheritance. Even when reared independently, if one twin has depression, the other twin is likely to develop it as well.

Brain chemistry and depression

Mind and body are both affected by depression. Recent advances in imaging techniques that map brain activity have enabled scientists to develop new perspectives in understanding the complexity of the brain and its chemistry, but much remains unknown.

The brain is frequently compared to a battery and when it is charged emotions are cheerful and stable but when it goes flat, instability occurs. To keep the brain battery firing, the correct chemical balance is necessary.

The brain contains special chemicals to keep in balance. The brain chemicals are called neurotransmitters and they transmit messages that enable connections between neurons or nerve cells throughout the brain. The three main neurotransmitters involved are, serotonin, norepinephrine (noradrenaline) and dopamine. Basically the neurotransmitters regulate moods, sleep, and appetite. Mood becomes low when the brain is unable to access the sufficient and correct levels of the combined necessary neurotransmitters.

Changes in the levels of these chemicals is closely linked to your particular physiology, the way you view the world, your personality, environmental factors, and heredity. Hopefully laboratories will be encouraged to continue their research to develop superior treatments for depression in the near future.

Hormones

Imbalance in the body's hormones can affect brain chemicals. Corticotropin-Releasing-Factor (CRF) is one of the neurohormones that regulates your body's reaction to stress. During severe stress or a perceived threat, the area of your brain controlling stress hormones, the hypothalamus, responds by releasing an increase of the hormones in the pituitary gland and adrenal glands. The "fight flight response" is then initiated and a person is prepared to fight, defend themselves or flee.

The mind becomes extremely alert and aware, breathing is shallower and muscles tense. Studies have shown that when excessive CRF floods the system due to constant stress, depression can follow. Some antidepressant medications have been specifically designed to lower CRF levels.

Female hormones are often associated with depression. Childbirth, the menstrual period and menopause are times in a woman's life when she is most vulnerable to depression. Not only during these times of hormonal change but very often the addition of associated stress, can plummet a woman into depression. Many women suffering from biochemical hormonal reactions have been helped with the appropriate medical treatment.

Medical conditions

The conditions that can create chemical changes that may cause depression are the following:

- Some forms of cancer.

- Heart failure and heart attack.

- Adrenal and pituitary abnormalities.

- Hormonal disorders like Cushing's syndrome, a condition that results from a tumour on the pituitary gland.

- Infectious illnesses, especially viral infections.

- Neurological conditions such as Alzheimer's disease; multiple sclerosis, Parkinson's disease, stroke, and brain injury.

- Hormones produced by the thyroid gland can affect depression. An over-active thyroid is likely to cause anxiety and insomnia while an underactive thyroid can result in feeling tired, slow and even depressed.

- Malnutrition and severe vitamin deficiencies can also contribute to depression.

Sleep-wake rhythms

Any disruption to your sleep routine can affect the way you feel and function the next day. Researchers have found that people who are depressed have characteristic disturbances in their sleep patterns. They often wake during the night and early morning and tend to spend less time than normal in restorative deep sleep and more time in dream sleep or rapid eye movement (REM) sleep. They also enter REM sleep earlier than is usual. Whether depression is the cause of these disruptions to sleep cycles, or if a disturbed sleep-wake cycle contributes to it, remains uncertain at this stage.

Seasonal changes

The mating and hibernation cycles of animals are affected by the available sunlight in the changing seasons. Like some animals, we humans react to variations in the amount of sunlight available. On dull winter days, the decrease in light is thought to trigger depression in some people.

Seasonal affective disorder (SAD), often known as the "winter blues", is more common in cold countries far from the equator. If you have SAD you may feel anxious, hopeless and negative about the future, sleep far more than usual, but still feel exhausted and eat much more than you do during summer. Although rare, summer depression can occur.

Researchers have tied changes in brain chemistry in people with depression, to seasonal variations in the chemical messenger serotonin. As a result of links found between exposure to bright light and serotonin, bright light therapy was developed to ease depression. It is given daily for about thirty minutes, while the person is seated in front of a specially designed box that radiates full-spectrum fluorescent light fitted with a diffusing screen. Many people with SAD respond well to this treatment alone or together with antidepressant medication.

The mind-body connection

Some people who suffer from physical ill health have an underlying emotional disorder such as depression. Often they can't pinpoint the cause of their distress. Depression can be masked and therefore missed when it presents itself physically, with symptoms such as headaches, muscle pains and sleep disruption. Emotions are experienced physically as well as mentally. As a result of this mind-body interaction, the ripple effect of depression registers throughout the body.

After exhaustive physical tests which prove negative, your doctor may conclude that your basic problem is depression. You may feel so convinced that you have contracted some dangerous disease or that there are other physical origins to your ailments, that you seek other medical opinions, which are likely to return the same diagnosis.

Case study

After visiting several specialists who had found no answers to Jacqui's aches and pains, she was referred to me by her doctor. She spoke to me about her condition:

"I am tired and listless and have no energy. I'm never without an ache or pain somewhere in my body and have these awful headaches like a tight band across my forehead. I have felt down and physical health isn't that good. I've had 'flu twice this winter and if anything's going around, I'll catch it. I just don't seem able to fight off the bugs like I used to."

Her doctor told her that her immunity was probably low and that she ought to make sure to have enough rest and to try to sleep for eight hours.

"Months ago my doctor suggested that I have counselling, but I suppose I wasn't ready then."

How depression affects the immune system

When you become depressed, you undergo extensive changes in your nervous system, hormone levels, the functioning of neurotransmitters in your brain, and your immune system. These changes occur as the body attempts to defend itself against these unwelcome stresses.

The immune system is the major mechanism controlling the body's defence against disease and infection by identifying and destroying agents such as viruses, bacteria, parasites and fungi. It can distinguish between organisms from within the body and outside, and it will attempt to reject all external threats. This intricate system is able to record past experiences, so that if you had measles or chicken pox as a child, you will be protected from another bout in later life.

We have all experienced times when we've been emotionally stressed, physically exhausted or depressed and fallen victim to colds, sinusitis or urinary tract infections and other health problems, more readily than usual. If you are depressed, it is always best to discuss your medical history and your symptoms with your doctor.

FIVE

PSYCHOLOGICAL CAUSES OF DEPRESSION

Your personality defines who you are, your unique characteristics, beliefs, style of thinking, the way you interact with others and how you interpret and respond to life's experiences.

The way you think, your problem solving and coping strategies in particular, determines your vulnerability to depression. Some of your personality characteristics may put you at risk of developing depression. Review the following aspects of personality. Understanding and acknowledging your own personality characteristics will provide you with the insight to make positive changes:

- Self-esteem.

- Control, power and responsibility.

- Avoidance.

- Being in touch with your feelings and physical reactions.

- Connecting with others.

- Supportive relationships.

- Flexibility.

- Expectations.

Self esteem

Accepting and liking who you are as a person and acknowledging your skills, strengths and weaknesses, allows you to cope with all sorts of difficulties you may encounter, and any criticism, or rejection without blaming yourself unduly.

If you have low self-esteem you will be inclined to feel inferior to others, play down your positive qualities and see yourself in a negative light. If things don't go as you hoped, you may blame yourself instead of looking at the wider picture and taking into account other people's actions or outside forces. You may not take credit for your achievements and assume that luck played the major part in your success.

Control, power and responsibility

Being in control creates a sense of ease and content. It is not surprising that the issue of control has a profound impact on depression. Depression is often accompanied by feelings of helplessness and inadequate control of outcomes. Feelings of being responsible for far too much are another aspect of control. These extremes of control manifest themselves in the following ways.

If you are depressed you may be pessimistic, feel helpless and stuck, unable to change the path of your life. You may believe that bad experiences are your lot in life and that you are powerless to make changes. To protect yourself, you may become afraid of being optimistic and blame yourself for any misfortunes. As a result, you may become increasingly passive, accepting and unwilling to take any risks.

At the other end of the scale, desperation may lead you to attempt to control people and situations through careful strategies or special manipulations. The planning involves a great deal of thought and emotional investment. However, the more you imagine you are able to control life's events, the more frustrated and let down you will feel if you discover that this plan is unrealistic.

Avoidance

If you are a person who feels sensitive to criticism and rejection you are likely to find interacting with others and maintaining relationships difficult. You might feel socially inept and shy and anxiously study people for signs of approval. Due to these feelings you might try to avoid feeling stressed or unhappy by pretending all is well, try to escape by endless activities or try to block out your feelings or forget instead of facing the issues bothering you. Avoiding difficult or upsetting situations, places and people that you predict might make you uncomfortable may make your life more restrictive. Your confidence and sense of mastery and control may decrease.

Avoidance may take the form of illicit drugs, alcohol use or your involvement in excessive sex, all common methods of blocking out feelings. The avoidance cycle could eventually lead to a depressive episode or prolong the condition if you become severely stressed.

Being in touch physically and emotionally

Emotions are part of you and a constant presence underlying everything you do. Being emotionally aware means recognising your feelings and understanding why you feel a certain way. You need to express your feelings as well as understand the link between your feelings, thoughts and actions. If you are emotionally aware you will also understand the feelings of others and be able to empathise with them.

Your body gives you signals such as tiredness after a long walk. In the same way, your feelings are the signals of what is occurring in your life. Feeling frustrated, upset or angry is a signal that all is not well. Emotions underlie every aspect of your life and all that you do. They cannot be escaped or overlooked by blocking them or denying their existence. The body and mind are so interconnected that if your emotions are blocked you are unlikely to feel physically or emotionally well.

Connecting with others

If you are depressed you are likely to reserve your limited energy for the most essential elements of your life, such as work and caring for yourself and family members. The activities that once gave you pleasure, entertained you or gave you a sense of achieving are often put aside. Your connection with people that was once a part of life tends to lessen as you struggle to cope. Often the concern that they might notice that you aren't as well as you once were, have lost or gained weight may be a concern. The mere effort of having a conversation with healthy people who are interested and involved in their lives can become too much to bear. As a result ,you withdraw more and more and reduce the valuable areas of support available. Being socially involved creates an important balance and helps you to feel in contact with your world.

Supportive relationships

Often depression eats away at trust and may make you feel a burden to others. Being able to confide in a partner, relative or close friend may help you through this tough period. Feeling loved, accepted and cared for helps to strengthen your sense of security and purpose.

Flexibility

People who are relaxed with a flexible approach to life are less likely to become depressed than those who are rigid and tense. If you are insistent on following known and tested traditions or the single approach you have always used to solve a problem, you will reduce your ability to cope with life. Being a black and white thinker who can't see the middle ground and who constantly seeks routine or a pattern to follow, will make you less able to cope with difficulties in your life. Adaptability is the key to survival.

Expectations

If you have realistic expectations of how well you can make progress or achieve at work, in your relationship and other activities, you are likely to be contented. If you have high expectations of yourself you are likely to have to expect too much from others. However, unrealistically high expectations can cause you to be disappointed and lose self-esteem. If you are susceptible due to your hereditary or biological background, this could increase your chance of becoming depressed.

HOW WE DEVELOP OUR VIEW ABOUT OURSELVES

Childhood experiences

To a large extent, the way you think about yourself, others and the world around you shapes your personality. Your view of yourself develops mainly at an early age through the beliefs and values your parents passed on to you, as well as the way you were treated by them. Their way of expressing their love and their means of discipline shaped the person you are today. Losses or traumas experienced during your childhood may have influenced you as well as peers, colleagues, teachers and other significant people you encountered.

If you were taught constructive positive attitudes by your parents and they provided you with support and genuine affection, you are more likely to be well equipped to deal with life. However, if you are not as fortunate, and your view of yourself is more negative than positive and you were not given the support and security you needed, try to realise that most parents do the best they can. Unfortunately, those parents who have experienced a deprived, hurtful or unloving childhood themselves do not have the emotional resources to give their own children all that is necessary to grow and develop a positive self-image.

If you have suffered during your childhood, it is natural to feel deprived, hurt or resentful. It is easy to offer suggestions to reduce the hurts of the past, and it is likely many suggestions have been offered before. As intense and deep as many of those hurts are and as painful as memories may be, try to find some way of moving on or seeking help. Severe emotional pain doesn't disappear. It festers inside and may increase your likelihood of developing depression or it could prolong existing depression.

Case study

Jane, an only child, grew up quiet and withdrawn. She had frequently been told she "wasn't very bright". No matter how hard she tried she could not please her parents. Her family was poor and her father regularly struggled to pay the rent. There were times when she overheard him tell her mother that he wished they didn't have a child – that she was a burden.

Jane believed she was a failure, unworthy and unlovable. Nothing her mother said to her made up for what she had heard. Any signs of criticism she noticed in her parents or others made her anxious and defensive.

When Jane married Ted their relationship appeared to be loving and affectionate. Though he gave her no reason to feel ill at ease, she was constantly anxious, fearing that Ted would leave, find someone else. If he stayed back late at work her security was shaken and she panicked, imagining he was having an affair. Jane confronted him regularly, until eventually he could no longer stand her accusations and left her for his accommodating secretary. Jane brought about the rejection she feared. Her self-esteem crumpled, her anxiety escalated and then she became depressed. Though she struggled with self-esteem, counselling helped her put her past into perspective.

She and Ted are separated but they have begun to talk to each other again and there is hope of reconciliation.

Life events

Life events have impact on your personality and how you deal with stress provoking events throughout your life. If faced with unusual or unpredictable changes, vulnerable individuals can be tipped into depression. Some of these typically stressful events that cause stress are:

- The death of a spouse.
- Separation from a partner or divorce.
- Imprisonment.
- Death of a close family member.
- Personal injury or illness.
- Dismissal from work.
- A new baby and moving house.

Modern life has become fast and at times frenetic. The family unit is breaking down, divorce is increasing, job tenure is often insecure and work is more demanding and pressured. Lack of time and tiredness affects mutual support and closeness in relationships. Our reliance is turning more and more towards technology. With the internet we no longer need to join the crowds to do our shopping. In so many ways, we are moving away from each other, becoming less connected, expressing and sharing fewer of our feelings, hopes and needs. Many people feel isolated.

We all get pushed to the limit from time to time. Stress can be positive, keep you focussed and improve your performance. Being constantly on edge due to excessive or prolonged stress whether it's due to a positive event such as preparing for marriage or a chronic, long and sad situation such as caring for a dying relative, may make you vulnerable to depression.

Your body prepares you to cope with emergencies or periods of intense focus but sustained or excessive stress may result in elevated cortisol levels. Cortisol which has earned the name of the stress hormone is secreted by your adrenal glands in response to signals from the hypothalamus in your brain. If you are undergoing chronic stress your levels of cortisol are likely to be higher than normal. Fortunately your body's stress response is usually self-regulating and once a perceived threat passes, cortisol levels drop and your system should return to normal.

Most people cope with stress in their lives without becoming depressed. It is unlikely that stress alone can cause depression. A depressive episode may be the culmination of years of struggling to cope with a combination of issues.

Developmental stages

Each one of us passes through a number of developmental stages in a lifetime. For some of us a specific stage can be particularly stressful. Adolescence, marriage, a first child, menopause and old age are all such stages. Information about depression occurring during these stages is discussed later in this book.

Are men or women more vulnerable to depression?

Men and women express their experience of depression differently. While in general, women tend to be more open and verbal about their depression, men often try to maintain outward control and withdraw from family, friends and workmates.

If you are a man, the macho stereotype of stoic acceptance and unflinching bravery in the face of pain or adversity may be a pattern that you have been reared to follow. If your depression is so severe that you are forced to seek help there is often an outpouring of years of stored, wounded emotions.

Depression is almost twice as common in women as in men. Women are more prone to hormonal changes that affect their moods. If you are a woman you may have grown up with the traditional belief that you are one of the caregivers and homemakers in society. Along with many other women, you may be caught in a bind, enjoying a caring role, but needing to compete in the male-dominated workforce for financial reasons or to advance a career. Struggling to manage with work pressures, home responsibilities, nurturing children, maintaining a marriage and often looking after elderly relatives, can create intolerable stress that may make you susceptible to depression.

Is change possible?

The way you think, your attitudes and beliefs shape your personality and its characteristics. They have become your way of coping with life. However, if you make changes to your style of thinking, some of these characteristics can begin to change. Insight into the dysfunctional aspects of your personality, and understanding its importance can assist you in preventing depression.

SIX

CHANGES IN WOMEN THAT MAY TRIGGER DEPRESSION

Universally, women are about twice as likely as men to suffer from depression. There are many theories that attempt to explain this higher incidence of depression in women. Studies show that as well as biological factors, psychological and social factors are implicated.

Biological and hormonal causes of depression in women

Between menstruation and menopause women undergo several hormonal changes as preparation for the important role of motherhood. They are especially prone to depression during times of biological change, such as during the premenstrual, postnatal phases and later in menopause. Scientists are exploring how the cyclical rise and fall of oestrogen and other hormones associated with depressive illness may affect the brain chemistry.

Premenstrual syndrome (PMS)

In the two weeks preceding a menstrual period 30% to 50% of women experience PMS symptoms of fluid retention, food cravings (mainly sweets and carbohydrates), breast tenderness, joint pain, headaches and bloating. If you are depressed you might become more irritable, tense, tearful, and lethargic and notice changes in appetite and sleep patterns. As the symptoms of depression and the symptoms of PMS are similar and can overlap, telling them apart is often difficult.

Case study

Diane is a school teacher. She was feeling exhausted and having severe premenstrual problems after a year of trying to cope with her job and her role as a mother and housekeeper.

She burst into tears and then said, "About a week before my period I feel these changes in my body as if some alien creature has found a way of tormenting me. Tender breasts and bloating make me very uncomfortable. What's worse, I get an overwhelming sad feeling as I get near to my period. It's a kind of loneliness that makes me cry. I'm so tense and agitated most of the time that I don't know what to do with myself. I'm self-critical too. I hate myself and my bloated body. Why do we women always have to suffer?"

During this premenstrual phase Diane had most of her arguments with her husband. He told her that she was easy to get along with the rest of the month but he was forced to "walk on egg shells" around her during this time and that any little thing upset her.

After several individual sessions with Diane, we worked out ways that would allow her to relax more and cope during the premenstrual phase. It involved a great deal of planning. She did as much of her shopping and administrative tasks for school in the weeks prior to this phase. She also set aside as much time as she could to be with her children.

In a joint session her husband agreed to help with last minute shopping, some extra chores and cooking at this time. Admittedly, it took a lot of organisation but with the support of her family, Diane felt less stressed and everyone benefitted.

Pregnancy

Most women feel emotionally well during pregnancy, however extreme stress can make a woman vulnerable to depression. These are some of the stresses that might precipitate depression during pregnancy:

Relationship issues

- Sexual intimacy can become a stressful issue. As a pregnancy develops many mothers-to-be feel unattractive and don't want to be touched.

- Some fathers-to-be are afraid that sexual activity might harm the baby. This attitude can make some mothers-to-be feel unloved and unattractive.

- The financial burden of supporting a child can create a great deal of stress.

- Difficulties in communicating can build up on both sides and result in stress.

- If the father of the expected child is no longer involved with the mother-to-be, or her close relatives have declared their lack of interest in her or the child she is carrying, stress is likely to occur.

Difficulties during pregnancy

- Resenting the pregnancy or not wanting the child at this time.

- If the expectant mother is having severe morning sickness or other health problems related to the pregnancy.

- The hormonal changes that occur during pregnancy may increase a woman's anxiety so that she could be more vulnerable to feelings of panic and severe stress.

- If a pregnancy is complicated or involves risk, this can take its toll on an expectant mother, particularly if she has to undergo several procedures and tests.

- Necessary bed rest prevents a woman from involving herself in her usual routine and can result in restlessness and stress.

- Any fears about the unborn child's safety or the birth process may escalate her fears.

Life events affecting pregnancy

A number of circumstances may occur during pregnancy that predisposes a mother-to-be to depression. These are important life changes, such as:

- Divorce or separation.
- Illness or death of a close relative.
- The loss of a job.
- Moving house.
- Financial constraints.

Infertility or loss in a previous pregnancy

The struggle to become pregnant, a miscarriage or the sadness of loss of a child in a past pregnancy might make you extremely anxious and prone to depression.

Postpartum (postnatal, perinatal) depression

For most parents the birth of a new baby is a joyous event, even if it is demanding and tiring. Parents struggle to cope with the new baby's needs, manage their own sleep deprivation and the changes in their routine. While most parents cope well, some have difficulty adjusting.

According to the Deloitte Access Economics report 2012, which was commissioned by The Post and Antenatal Depression Association (PANDA), 1 in 7 new mums and 1 in 20 new dads are diagnosed with postnatal depression annually. The estimates are that healthcare costs decreased productivity and forgone tax will cost Australia $433 million in 2012.

The following factors are found to be associated with a risk of postpartum depression:

- Depression in pregnancy.
- A dramatic drop in oestrogen and progesterone after childbirth.
- Anxiety in caring for the new baby.
- Sleep deprivation.
- A very demanding baby.

- Difficulty breast feeding.
- Older sibling jealousies.
- A past history of depression.
- A family history of depression.
- Lack of family support.
- Severe stress.

Case study

It was Beth and Jeremy's first child and she wasn't coping with her baby at all well.

"When I found out that I was pregnant I was thrilled but I was sick in the early months and then heavy and uncomfortable. The tiny creature that emerged was so strange – red and wrinkly that I couldn't believe he was mine. I can't say that I loved him at first sight. I knew it wasn't how I was supposed to feel. I should have been ecstatic about having a baby, but somehow I wasn't. And I struggled with my milk."

She sighed. "Breast-feeding may be the most natural thing in the world but it wasn't for me. I felt self-conscious feeding him. On the fourth day I started to cry, and I didn't know why. The nurses smiled and said I had baby blues, that is was very common and that it would go soon."

Beth wiped away a few tears with her tissue. "My down moods came and went for a few weeks, and now I'm feeling sad every day. I wonder if I'll ever feel happy again."

Once she had seen her doctor and begun taking an antidepressant, Beth's mood improved. She had stopped breast feeding, so that there would be no concerns about the medication affecting the baby. With the help of a child care nurse and regular counselling sessions as well, she recovered soon.

Once the baby was eighteen months old she put him in a crèche and returned to work. The stimulation of work was her greatest help. In her last counselling session she said, "I'm not going to have another child. One will have to be enough. I don't want to go through all that misery again."

Instead of the joy that many new mothers expect to feel after having a baby, the hormonal changes after childbirth can cause profound mood changes.

The forms of postpartum (postnatal depression, perinatal) depression

Depression, the most common type of emotional disorder affecting new mothers, can occur in three forms: baby blues, postnatal depression and postpartum psychosis.

Baby blues

About two to four days after childbirth many new mothers experience baby blues, with one or more of these symptoms: crying, emotional reactions, anger, irritability, insomnia, restlessness, tension and exhaustion. After two weeks the blues have usually disappeared.

Postnatal depression

Unlike the sudden onset of the baby blues, postnatal depression develops slowly and is often accompanied by mood swings. This form of depression can affect up to one-quarter of new mothers. It usually occurs within the first six weeks after childbirth but it may appear at any time during the baby's first year. A new mother with postnatal depression may experience some of the following symptoms:

- Depression, which may occur with mood swings.
- Severe anxiety, which may escalate to panic.
- Crying spells and tearfulness.
- Lack of interest in the new baby.
- Changes in sleep patterns – sleeping more, less, or broken sleep.
- Extreme changes in appetite – overeating or lack of appetite.
- Guilt about depressive feelings, as giving birth is meant to be a joyous time.
- Agitation and irritability.

- Obsessive thoughts about the child.
- Lack of concentration and forgetfulness.
- Suicidal thoughts.

Factors that may contribute to depression include:
- An inability to adjust to the motherhood role.
- The loss of a career and personal freedom.
- Changes that having a new baby bring to a relationship with a partner.
- Feelings of inadequacy as a mother.
- Inability to live up to expectations of motherhood.
- Fatigue may be overwhelming.
- A new mother may fear she will be unable to cope emotionally with the demands of her role.
- If support is lacking, she will experience even more difficulties.

Treatment for postnatal depression

If you are a mother suffering from postnatal depression do not be afraid to tell your doctor if you are not coping with the demands of motherhood or that you are depressed. Talking about how you feel can be both reassuring and helpful. Your partner will also need some help in understanding your situation and it might be a good idea to include him occasionally when you visit the doctor. Antidepressant therapy is commonly prescribed by doctors if your depression is severe. It is likely that you will also need counselling to rebuild your self-esteem and to help you to relax with your new baby.

Postpartum psychosis

This extreme condition may occur approximately a month after childbirth. It is a serious illness, usually in women with a biological predisposition to depression, and takes the form of severe mood swings similar to those of bipolar disorder. The new mother may also have delusions and believe her baby is damaged in some way or possessed by evil forces. She may even attempt to hurt or harm herself and the baby.

This condition is thought to be triggered by extreme stress. The stress needs to be dealt with immediately and women assisted with the life changes a baby brings. Whether control issues, difficulties with a partner, memories of a horrific birth or fear of being locked in to a life of caring for the baby and loss of career, a woman suffering from this psychosis is in urgent need of assistance in the form of medication and psychological therapy and support.

Menopause

Menopause usually occurs between 45 and 55 and represents a dramatic turning point for women emotionally, physically and intellectually. It is literally a change of life. For approximately 80 per cent of women the cessation of their periods and the transition to menopause brings hardly any discomfort. Only a relatively small number have symptoms severe enough to require medical attention.

Most common signs of menopause

- Hot flushes, night sweats.
- Loss of libido.
- Crawling or itching sensations under the skin.
- Fatigue.
- Headaches.
- Urinary frequency.
- Vaginal dryness.
- Weight gain.

Case study

Trish walked into the room dragging her feet, her hair was uncombed, her eyes swollen and red from crying. She sighed loudly as she sank into the chair. It was the third time she had come for counselling.

"I was up most of the night and had to shower and change my nightgown twice because of drenching sweats," she complained. "My thermostat must be wrecked, because I'm either boiling or freezing. I've never been so crabby and uptight in my life. Who'd want to be a woman going through menopause?"

She moved around restlessly and then looked up. "Last week you asked me to write down the things that were bothering me. Well I've got a long list." She felt in her handbag for her glasses. "First of all there's my elderly father. He's in a retirement village, but he might as well be on my doorstep. I visit him every second day, but he wants more and more of me until there's nothing left. Then, John and I have a business. I do all the bookwork and between that, the housekeeping, cooking and cleaning. There's my daughter who wants me to baby-sit." She thumped the arm of the chair. "I haven't got a moment to myself. I know that I have to draw the line somewhere and say "no", but I can't."

We talked about her becoming more assertive and then moved on to the subject of hormone replacement. "I haven't been on HRT yet and I'm not quite sure if I should go on it," she said. "The doctor says he'll put me on it for a short while, but `there are so many different views about it. My friends who have been through menopause tell me that eventually the unpleasant symptoms settle down and you start to feel healthy and energised again. But, I don't know...I'll have to think hard about it. I'd like to sort out my problems and tablets won't do it all for me. I want to emerge from the menopause in one piece, ready to face the rest of my life."

In her book *The Silent Passage*, Gail Sheehy writes about misinformation and the stigma of ageing in a youth orientated society: She maintains that women's fears are: "I'll lose my looks, I'll lose my sex appeal. I'll get depressed, fade into the woodwork, I'll become invisible." Sheehy maintains that women don't have to lose any of these things.

You, like many other women may respond to the ageing process with fear of future deterioration. Growing older may mean a rush to the hairdresser to colour greying hair, dieting or joining a gym to keep a youthful figure. This is also the time of life when you may encounter additional responsibilities and difficulties. Notable are, caring for aged parents or facing the death of a parent, coming to terms with your partner's retirement or retrenchment, and coping with adult or nearly adult children who may be an emotional or financial drain.

Depression is more likely to occur if you have experienced a recent bereavement, a traumatic event, a surgically induced menopause, if you have been depressed before or if there is a family history of depression. Being under severe stress or carrying too heavy an emotional load at this time can compound the situation or even trigger depression if you are predisposed to it.

Treatment available for menopausal relief

For most women, friends are a great support at this time but if symptoms become severe, fortunately medical help is available in the form of hormone replacement therapy (HRT) which corrects the imbalance of oestrogen in your body. If you are severely depressed your doctor may also prescribe antidepressant medication.

If you prefer to use a *natural therapy*, Dr Sandra Cabot, well-known writer, naturopath and medical doctor, advocates eating foods that contain plant oestrogens, such as linseeds, soya milk and beans, oats, rice, parsley, alfalfa and chickpeas. She also suggests taking herbs that stimulate the body's natural production of oestrogen. These include sage, black cohosh, wild yam, red clover, sarsaparilla and liquorice. Always consult a naturopath or herbalist for advice before self-medicating.

Don't forget that help is available in the form of counselling to assist you in coping with the difficulties involved in this transition.

In spite of problems with adjustment, the occasional mood swings and down days, most women pass through this phase unscathed.

SEVEN

CHANGES IN MEN THAT MAY TRIGGER DEPRESSION

Men and women are affected differently by depression. Men tend to focus on the physical symptoms of depression rather than the emotional ones, such as tiredness and irritability, losing their temper and feeling angry. They may also complain of headaches, irritability, sleep difficulties or sexual problems. In the same way as women, they might lose interest in activities, they once enjoyed and withdraw from former social activities but they are less likely than women to talk about the way they feel. Often they do not seek help from their doctors. Instead many men throw themselves into their work for longer hours, try to escape by activity or tend to drink more in the hope of drowning their unhappiness. Therefore it is not surprising that depression often goes undiagnosed in men.

Like many other men, you may have been reared with an emphasis on self-control and were taught that enduring difficulties rather than being weak by showing your true feelings was the manly way. And so you may have remained stoic and tried to suppress your unhappiness or even despair. Even if you've been aware of your depression, you might've tried to mask it, hoping it will disappear. Like so many, you may be afraid that if others find out about your condition it will adversely affect your work situation or your standing in the community and your children may lose respect for you.

Unfortunately many of these views are based on false premises and held by many men even in our modern times. As a result, a number of men do not seek the treatment that would help them to recover quickly.

The role of stress

Stress plays a key role in male depression. Men and boys of all ages go through major life changes or events that may trigger depression such as:

- Stress at work (at school or home).
- Parents' divorce.
- Concerns about sexuality.
- Verbal, physical, or sexual abuse.
- Failing to meet the standard required (a test, exam or goal set by an organisation).
- Dropping out of school early.
- A stressful first job (college, university or military service).
- Unemployment.
- Being unable to reach the goals set.
- Financial problems of all sorts (including gambling debts).
- Frequent change of jobs.
- Moving or leaving home for the first time.
- Relationship problems.
- Being away from friends and family.
- The death of a loved one.
- A serious illness, accident or injury.
- Starting a family.
- Family responsibilities such as caring for children, a spouse/partner, or ageing parents.
- Retirement.
- Illness in old age, financial or other difficulties.

Fathers and depression

There is a great deal of information about how mothers cope after the birth of a child but until recently little information has been available about a new father's reaction to a first baby. In an analysis of over a large sample of 3000 fathers participating in the Growing Up in Australia: Longitudinal Study of Australian Children (LSAC), it was discovered that approximately one in ten fathers report high levels of distress in the first year after having a baby.

If you are a new father woken during the night by a baby's cries, you may allow your partner to grab extra sleep and get up to change a nappy or settle the baby down. If there are other children in the family, frequently you feed them, make sure they're ready for school and drive them there. After work you may stop at a supermarket. There is no doubt that your routine is disrupted and your responsibilities increased. According to the study, stress of a new baby is heightened if your work situation is insecure and working hours inflexible. You may need to be at home and have to flexible.

With a new baby at home, your relationship with your partner will change significantly. The demands of caring for the baby means that you will spend less time together. Arguments about parenting approaches and issues of jealousy over the new baby may also come into play and other issues may arise.

The topic of family stress is immense and cannot be covered in this general book on depression.

Mid-life changes in males (Mid-life crisis)

Most men cope well during the years between 40 and 60 and enjoy a general slowing down, but for some this stage can be more challenging. Apart from the responsibilities and stresses of day to day living, midlife can be an uncomfortable time of introspection. Many men question the choices and decisions made earlier. Dissatisfaction with a lifestyle and boredom with people and activities previously of interest may occur. A sudden issue at work, home or financial difficulties may be the trigger for depression. For some men childhood issues that have not been dealt with sufficiently tend to surface at this time.

Your relationship with your partner will have changed and children may have left the nest or be about to leave. As a result, partners may become strangers, alone for the first time since before the children were born. Both have to work at a sagging relationship. Cravings for rekindled youth, excitement and stimulation can lead to sexual liaisons or activities that provide a thrill, such as driving fast cars, gambling, and hang gliding.

Case study

Don sat with his head in his hands. "Is that all there is?" he muttered. "Look at me, forty-one, losing my hair and what's left is starting to grey. I wear glasses and I'm spreading. Certainly nothing like I used to be."

He wasn't seeking a response and went on speaking. "Want to know why I feel empty most days? Well, I guess I've made it...struggled all my life, from the time I left school at sixteen, climbed the ladder rung by rung, clawed my way up, and now there's nothing left to look forward to."

I nodded and he continued, "I had a lot to overcome in my life...things I can't talk about now...by my uncle of all people. It's always there in the background, like a monkey on my back."

I tried to interrupt but he continued at a fast pace "Then there's my marriage. Anne and I were childhood sweethearts, but we've had nothing to talk to each other about for years. The kids kept us together but they've gone now and we're alone in an empty house. Sex is boring with no passion, so, maybe you can understand why Gloria came into my life. She's fifteen years younger, so I need to look my best."

"Let's slow down, look at what's happened in your life, stage by stage," I suggested.

"No. I just want to get on with things...maybe going away on a long overseas holiday will help me more."

The holiday did nothing for Don other than give him a sun tan. He was still depressed when I saw him again but this time he wanted to talk about it.

Is there a male menopause?

There is no conclusive scientific evidence to suggest that men undergo hormonal changes similar to a woman's at menopause. There are however, gradual changes in testosterone levels in the forties and sixties, which mainly have an impact on sexual functioning, and may cause impotence and lack of desire.

When men retire

Retirement is the period of life when most men can put their dreams and plans into action for the first time. You will have time to relax, travel, read or study, work in your garden or play a sport like golf or bowls. But for you, like many men, it may mean the lack of status and self-esteem. The stable routine you followed for most of your life and the purpose of a job is gone. If you have focussed all your attention and energy on your job this change can be stressful. Retirement can also bring financial problems with money being shorter than it once was.

If retirement is not a satisfying experience and there are no real challenges to meet, life can become dull and purposeless and depression could occur.

How men cope best with retirement

There is a lot of research to show that the men who cope best with retirement are those who stay active and involved. These are some suggestions:

- Developing an old hobby or starting a new one.
- Staying physically active, through walking, swimming, gym or sport. (Make sure your exercise routine is appropriate for your physical capacities and limitations).
- Volunteering with a charity or church group.
- Studying a course of interest.

PART 2

THE INNER ROUTE

EIGHT

THE INNER ROUTE

The healing power of stories

I've always enjoyed listening to stories about people's lives. Many stories were told to me by older people and some I read. Later I began to write my own stories taken from my observations and experiences. This collection of my tales is about depressed people. They are part of me and I've learned so much from writing them. Now I would like to share them with you.

The use of imagination and dreams in the stories will draw you away from your everyday experience, tickle your imagination in the hope of broadening your horizons and elicit meaningful growth. They will prompt associations with your own valuable memories, dreams or experiences, influencing your choices and the direction you take. Timing is an important factor. An idea in a story that may have been meaningless to you three months ago may help you to move forward now.

I am sure that you will find that the stories add a new dimension to your view on life, and you will enjoy reading them. If they don't suit your thinking style, bypass them and concentrate on the more rationally based cognitive techniques in the rest of the book.

The role of stories in the past

Stories have always been part of our lives and are ways of educating, entertaining or stimulating thought. We are used to stories being told by family members, reading or watching them performed on stage, television or in a movie.

The story was the earliest form of spreading knowledge, a way of accounting for historical events or a method of announcing current information. Stories helped to maintain society's traditions, spreading its morals and reinforcing cultural values. The early Egyptians wrote down their stories. The bible, more than 2,000 years old, contains some of the earliest stories and Greek and Roman myths are full of symbolic meaning. Later, minstrels travelled the countryside telling and singing stories while accompanying themselves on musical instruments.

Fairy tales, myths, parables and fables are common to most cultures and have always been favourites. They have messages and describe solutions to a variety of predicaments. The most popular stories that have survived the years are those in which good triumphs over evil or the underdog becomes the victor as in Cinderella or the Ugly Duckling. Storytelling plays an essential part in healing in indigenous cultures. Healing stories are usually about the important values to those cultures and help individuals to find their place in their group. Many current stories continue to tell us about aspects of our lives, ways of overcoming difficulties and making sense of our lives.

Stories that change the way you think and feel

We can be so used to our way of thinking, feeling and doing things that we are almost programmed to continue in that way. But if we allow ourselves to look at our world differently, through another window, we might gain new insights. Stories can offer us a new perspective, a new way out of a mental trap.

While the rest of this book boosts your knowledge, provides your rational mind with the information and strategies you need to combat depression, these stories will further stimulate your recovery by nourishing your inner world with insight and inspiration. Focusing on relieving your despair though your rational, external world is not enough. What about your inner world of dreams, imagination, fantasy and memories? It offers you a wealth of possibilities for beating your depression and should never be diminished or ignored.

These stories are there for you, while you work on changing the quality of your thinking and feeling. They are *not* designed to be used instead of traditional forms of treatment for depression, but rather to equip you with an additional weapon in your fight. The information you gain about your depression in the rest of the book will be reinforced by any changes you make as a result of reading these tales.

The unconscious

The unconscious discussed here is not Freud's unconscious of repressed drives and urges, or Jung's mythical symbolism. It refers to all those thoughts, feelings and perceptions beyond your awareness. Your unconscious has much to offer you. It is a source of creativity, tapped by artists, poets and writers over the centuries.

Without realising it, you use your unconscious every day to help you with skilled activities that have become automatic, like riding a bicycle, driving a car, or using a dishwasher or computer. The way a memory can pop up out of nowhere, a feeling surface without summoning it, and intuitive awareness of danger tap you on the shoulder, is due to your unconscious. When you 'sleep on' an idea to provide an answer, you are locking into your unconscious.

Renowned psychotherapist Milton Erickson believed that the unconscious could provide solutions to turn a situation around or ignite change. The stories he told his patients appealed to their unconscious minds, encouraging learning and change. He believed that we all have the ability and resources to stimulate recovery.

To access the riches of your unconscious, be flexible and open, listen to your intuition. If a story appeals to you, ask yourself why. If a story strikes a chord within you, examine it more deeply and read the relevant passages again. Allow yourself to be receptive to the tales that touch you.

Dreams

Dreams are as natural and as much part of your life as walking or breathing. They are internal messages that provide you with feedback on how you feel. Your dreams help you to access the data bank of your memory and provide links with your inner world. Freud called dreams the "royal road to the unconscious". They process information experienced during the day and provide insight into troublesome situations in your life. Dreams may bring solutions to problems and without them you may be unaware of many of your thoughts and feelings.

In the stories, dreams are frequently used to resolve problems. The dreamer recognises the value and importance of a dream even though the precise details may not be fully understood. The dreamers possess an openness to receive the message from within and make them part of daily experience.

Suggestions for reading the stories

- It is best to be relaxed while reading a story. Experiment with a relaxation exercise prior to reading, deep breathing or listening to gentle music.

- Select a story and read it at your own pace.

- Try to suspend your rational assessments and open your mind and heart to let in your imagination and creativity. You can approach problem solving with your total capacity not just your logical ability.

- Though the tales are easily understood and are about ordinary people, their effect on you can be profound. You may not notice much of a difference in the way you feel immediately after reading one and possibly dismiss it, but if it has a place in your recovery or growth, your unconscious will store it for later use. A day or two later or more you may find that you feel inspired to make a change in direction or you may be encouraged to try something novel. Whether you can connect the story with your action is unimportant. The most important thing is to move forward towards recovery.

A LIST OF STORIES IN THE BOOK

STORY	SUBJECT	PAGE
On Strike	A stressed, overworked woman whose family take her for granted.	page 68
Learning to Love	Depression in the family against a background of individual problems.	page 83
The Wheel of Fortune	A gambler who drinks excessively and has severe mood swings.	page 92
The Lake	A man learns about the value of friends and loved ones.	page 105
Search for Meaning	A depressed man's search for answers takes him to India.	page 113
Trapped	A prisoner becomes depressed. When he is released he creates his own prison.	page 120
The Winding River	A young woman's self-growth on her river journey.	page 131
The Blue Venetian Vase	A woman going through menopausal depression finds answers.	page 142
Looking for Trouble	When in difficult circumstances, a young woman meets an unusual character who helps her to balance her moods.	page 153
The Road to Recovery	How the love of a cat helps a depressed man with an alcohol addiction.	page 168
Letting Go	A middle aged woman begins to appreciate her value.	page 179
Family Treasures	A depressed young woman discovers her roots.	page 191
The Suit	How a depressed young man changes over time.	page 199
Imagination Fired	A severely depressed young woman is rekindled by her inner fire.	page 208
Beauty Within	A woman learns the value of relaxation and meditation in easing a down mood.	page 216
Mr Woody	A young person finds a way to handle school bullies.	page 252
Making Choices	A young man is helped to come to terms with past pain.	page 262
Partners	Through a crisis a couple are drawn closer together.	page 274
Ground Zero	Healing after a traumatic event.	page 285

Healing story: *On strike*

This is one of my favourite stories. It is about Margaret a woman worn out by work and frustrated by her family who took her for granted.

She observed the thick line of ants filing across the window ledge, over the shutter and down the wall, absorbed in their movements as they scurried behind each other.

That's me, just one of a number racing to keep going, Margaret thought and sighed. It would be another day at work, fitting in her household chores and insufficient time to spend with her children. It worried her that when they came home from school in the afternoon she wasn't giving them enough of her attention. That the house didn't meet her usual high standard of neatness and cleanliness bothered her too. So many things in her life had become responsibilities and obligations to others that she fulfilled without question. Over weekends she helped her husband with his accounts and a few days a week after work she squeezed in a visit to her father in hospital. The demands on her had taken their toll and at the end of the day she was so tired that she barely managed to cook the evening meal.

Her work had been enjoyable and she was a conscientious and efficient secretary until a new computer system was introduced. Not only were her records thrown into chaos but she was forced to learn a totally different approach to her work. Learning was slow and tedious and for the first time she dreaded work each day.

One Friday she decided to take a lunch break. She usually grabbed a sandwich and coffee and worked through lunch but this time she wanted to shake off a gloominess weighing her down. It was a warm day and the streets were throbbing with lunchtime shoppers. She passed elegant shops but didn't stop to look in their windows. Walking fast, she attempted to push away her doubts about the new computer system. When she reached her favourite cafe, she found an outside table and sat in the sunshine under a striped awning.

As she spooned up the froth of her cappuccino, she heard sounds of marching and loud hailers coming from a few blocks away. She gulped down her coffee and followed the sound. Members of the Garment Workers Union were on strike and the street was packed. She read the placards. *Put your money where your mouth is. You've sewn us up.* The large mob of protesting workers stomped and yelled their demands.

As a young woman, her mother had worked as a machinist in a factory and had told her about the strain of making every seam straight in the fastest possible time. Margaret nodded to herself. She knew how it felt to be undervalued, both at home and in her job. She watched the enthusiastic crowd and felt the throb of their excitement. In minutes, she was caught up in the mood of the march. Without thinking she joined in yelling with them. *Slave labour. Less time more money.* She rarely shouted and didn't display her feelings in public but this was different.

Well past lunch hour, the crowd surged past a tall building displaying a clock face. It was 2.20 p.m., but instead of heading back to the office she kept pace with the others. Finally the line of strikers thinned and a few stalwarts shook their placards at the crowd.

She clenched her fist. *I've had enough of being used by my family. Its time I did something about it...stood up for myself, showed them how I feel.* She made an instant decision, *I'm going on strike too.*

Margaret returned to the office. She complained of feeling ill and left for the day. In the bus home, waves of weariness swept over her as she sank into the seat. Tears of resentment dribbled down her cheeks and her legs were jelly during the brief walk from the bus stop to her house. She placed her handbag on the hall table and went into the bedroom. Her overriding need was to slip into bed. She closed her eyes and thought about her husband Dennis, who expected her to do all the housework and cooking as well as work. And then there were her two lazy teenage sons, usually sprawled out in front of the television, nibbling snack food.

Their vague offers to help in the house had been promised such a long time ago. She stretched and yawned. *It's time for them to take over. I'm not doing another thing. She smiled for the first time. Down go my household tools – iron, saucepan, vacuum, everything that cleans, cooks or chugs.*

In a dream sleep, her mother was standing before her, large and overbearing. Margaret was younger and small. "Lying around idle again, there's work to be done in the house, my girl. Get up!"

Meekly she followed her mother's instruction. "Come with me!" her mother said, as she walked around the house running her finger along glass tops and furniture. "This hasn't been dusted for days." Her mother straightened a few paintings and reorganised the cushions on the sofa before walking towards the door. "I'll leave you to it, then."

Margaret woke seething with resentment. *Why can't she can't leave me alone now that she's dead.*

When Dennis came home from work and found her in bed, he was stunned. He took one look at her pale face and called the doctor. Pulling a chair up to her bed, the doctor spoke kindly to her about looking after herself in the future. He told her that the stresses of working and caring for her home and her family would make her ill if she didn't rest. That she was having trouble sleeping and didn't have much appetite concerned him.

"A week off work and she's to stay in bed...then we'll see," he said to Dennis. "I want to see her in my surgery next Monday."

Dennis sat on the edge of the bed struggling to find words to tell her how worried he was and how much he cared. Later he brought her tea and roughly cut sandwiches. Between sobs she told him how tired she was and that for a while she couldn't face looking after him and the boys or the house. He had no idea where to start, but he wanted her to rest and promised that he and the boys would do their best.

That day and the next she lay in bed feeling drained, yet uncomfortable about relaxing. Lying in bed was foreign to her and she believed that women who gave in to minor illnesses were weak. Her mother visited her several times in dreams, always reprimanding her and each time she was filled with a mixture of guilt and resentment. During that week she slept more than she could remember. Even if she wanted to clean and cook her energy had deserted her. She felt guilty about not visiting her father in hospital too and phoned instead. Dennis and the boys applied themselves to most of the household chores. They mastered the dishwasher and vacuum cleaner, but struggled with sorting clothes for the washing machine. Dennis bought take-away food for two nights, and then longed for a solid meal. At the supermarket he bought frozen vegetables, chips and three huge slices of steak. She was astounded when he turned out a tasty meal. Dennis visited his father-in-law in hospital. Though it pleased her to see her men as they went about their chores, she feared that their dedication couldn't last.

When she saw the doctor again, he wasn't satisfied with her progress, muttered about mild depression, insisted on another week or two at home and offered her tablets to lift her mood.

She shook her head. *I'll get there on my own.* Gradually she left her bed, watched a little television and paged through magazines. The thought of returning to work made her apprehensive. Around that time Margaret had another dream about her mother. She had grown to almost adult size now and her mother's menacing comments no longer upset her.

"So what have you been doing all this time?"

"Resting Mother, it's what the doctor said I need to do."

"Humph", was the reply as her dead mother wandered round the house looking in corners and testing for dust. "Clean enough but not sparkling."

"It's time you left me to run my house," Margaret snapped. Miffed, her mother turned and walked off.

The dream amused her. She pictured her mother with a duster in one hand, a cleaning cloth in the other as she wiped surfaces with antiseptic or cleaned under furniture in a search for hidden dirt. The beds had to be made before she left in the morning and at least one load of washing done. Her mother hardly ever sat down and if she did it wasn't for long. It was the first time she had laughed or even smiled for weeks. Stronger and more optimistic, she began to enjoy her late sleeps, reading and occasional walks.

That weekend Dennis called a family meeting. There were hugs all round and expressions of pleasure about Margaret's improved health. Everyone agreed that before she considered returning to work a roster ought to be drawn up to share the responsibilities of managing the house. They insisted on taking on most of the home management between them and allotting her the remainder. The roster was to be reviewed as she grew stronger and was closer to her return to work. She was proud that Dennis was turning into an efficient housekeeper and her sons were taking an active part in running their home.

That night, she had her last dream about her mother. They were in her mother's sitting room having tea. Her mother appeared, white haired, small and frail, as she had been in her late seventies. They chatted pleasantly, and then kissed each other goodbye. She woke from that dream feeling relieved but sad at seeing her mother so weak.

When Margaret saw the doctor again he insisted on her staying at home for at least one more week. On her return, her boss and the office staff welcomed her. During her month away she had been missed and two replacement secretaries had been called in to do her job. The doctor had insisted she work for only a few hours in the morning and she kept to their agreement. Though she was home for a late lunch, exhaustion forced her to lie down most of the afternoon. Only later, she managed her few chores and then was forced to return to the bedroom.

After several weeks, work became easier and she no longer felt so tired in the afternoon. She decided not work a full day again. She wanted more time to herself and work that put her under less pressure. Her boss didn't want to lose her and was prepared to reduce her hours. The new computer system seemed less daunting and she mastered it in her own time, determined not to allow herself to become stressed again.

With her family helping out and less work pressure, her sense of humour and capacity to enjoy life returned. A plus was Dennis' new hobby, cooking. He had a natural flair and she couldn't believe her luck. On the days she worked, he cooked the meal. Soon she took over more household tasks, but not all of them. A good deal had been negotiated and she often wondered if the members of the Garment Workers Union had done as well with their strike.

PART 3

THE CONSTRUCTIVE ROUTE TO THINKING, FEELING AND ACTING

NINE
❧

HOW THINKING AFFECTS YOUR DEPRESSION

Each day you have thousands of thoughts. In a down mood, so many of your thoughts are negative and destructive. You may not realise that your mood is likely to have originated from your destructive thoughts or that depression begins with negative thinking. Most people assume that depression must be due to the way they feel. In order to heal your depression it is essential to understand the important role your thinking can play in generating and even deepening your depression.

The foundation of destructive thoughts

Many of your destructive thoughts existed long before you became depressed. Lack of self-esteem is built on a foundation of negative thinking and angry or resentful thoughts may stem from remembered early hurts or unfair treatment. Memories of an unhappy childhood or teenage years filled with insecurity and feelings of inadequacy are carried into adulthood and can form part of your thinking. Negativity can spread, making your efforts appear futile and the future look bleak.

How to change your thinking with the help of this book

You will find this book constructive and realistic in its approach. It will help you to identify those thoughts that pull you down and increase your depressive thinking. Then it will help you to learn to change those thoughts in a constructive manner to suit your own way of thinking and view of life. To achieve this, cognitive behavioural therapy (CBT) will form a key agent for change, but not the only one. There are healing tales interspersed between the chapters to enable you to increase your insight, as well as mindfulness-based cognitive therapy that can help you to break out of your depression.

COGNITIVE BEHAVIOURAL THERAPY (CBT)

This is a highly regarded, much researched and widely practiced form of therapy for treating depression and well suited for self-help. As a therapy, it has been proven to be effective on its own or together with medication. It is easy to master, works rapidly and results in positive mood changes.

CBT is based on the concept that the way our thoughts are formed and their content result in feelings of depression. It follows, that changing your destructive thoughts will allow you to free yourself from depression's grip. So it makes good sense to strive to develop a kinder and more productive style of thinking. These strategies will help you to do this on your own or with help from a friend or relative.

It will take you some time to cover the material in this part of the book thoroughly. Try to keep an open mind until you have completed reading it all. Afterwards you may return to sections you found most helpful.

Case study

Paul is 19, looking for a job and has an interview lined up. Although he is highly skilled and has excellent references, he is nervous. He imagines himself clamming up, going blank or saying the wrong things as was the case in previous interviews. Lying awake all night, he imagines the worst and feels so despondent that he thinks he'd be better off cancelling the interview. *I'm sure I'm going to make a mess of it. Better that I don't go, muck it up and just get upset.*

He lacks confidence in many other areas of his life as well, such as dating, making friends and playing sport. Women make him anxious and he rarely asks anyone out. *Why would a woman go out with me,* he tells himself, *I'm so boring and unattractive and I've got nothing special to offer.*

He can still hear his father bellowing, "You'll never pass your exams, and you haven't got what it takes." Underlying his insecurity and feelings of inadequacy are his unhappy experiences as a child feeling unloved, and later his struggles as a young man. "You should leave school as soon as possible." There were many more negative remarks his father made but he preferred not to think of them.

As hard as Paul tries he cannot get the thought that he is not worthwhile out of his head. He has been suffering from depression for almost eight months and though visits his doctor and is taking a mild antidepressant, his negative outlook doesn't shift. The doctor suggests counselling but he doesn't like the idea of talking to a stranger about the way he feels, and particularly about the past. *The past is better left buried,* he says to himself.

A few months later, Paul has not improved and is having trouble dragging himself out of bed after a night of interrupted sleep. He is barely eating and has not left the house. His mother is so concerned that she phones the doctor. Paul agrees to see his doctor again and finally visits a counsellor. Slowly he begins to work on his unproductive thinking. Over months he slowly recovers. He no longer minds talking to the counsellor. It is a relief to discuss things bottled up in his head and look at them logically.

IDENTIFYING DESTRUCTIVE THOUGHTS

One of the most constructive ways of fighting this onslaught of negativity is to teach yourself to identify and then challenge destructive thoughts.

We will examine the following patterns of destructive thinking:

1. Automatic thinking (self-talk)

2. Unreasonable beliefs

3. Destructive thinking styles

1. AUTOMATIC THINKING (SELF-TALK)

Automatic thinking, self-talk or self-dialogue, refers to those thoughts and feelings that seem to pop up in your pool of consciousness, providing ideas and obvious explanations of events. Some people know them as "the voice in my head". They occur so quickly, for no reason, that most of the time you are unaware that they underlie your thinking.

As they are your habitual way of thinking, they form your response to everyday demands. They don't allow for plans or options and let you to get on with your life as usual. They appear to be such comfortable ways of responding that they seem to be fact and reflect the truth. You may believe them for years until you have cause to confront them. You may even be unaware or forget that other people think differently and have a different view of life.

Of course your automatic thoughts can be positive and many of our warm and positive feelings about people, situations and events occur spontaneously. But when you are depressed, it is negative thoughts that swamp the positive ones and provide continuing feelings of distress.

Automatic thoughts may reflect your parents' or teachers' ideas or come from books, magazines, television and painful, hurtful experiences that have shaped your thinking. They form a core of powerfully destructive perceptions. Automatic thoughts can also occur in scenes you re-enact in your imagination to explain a situation to yourself. Sometimes they result from rehearsing what you may do or say in the future.

When automatic thoughts cause problems

When you are depressed your automatic thoughts are usually self-critical and fearful. You may not be aware that your automatic thinking is causing you to feel despairing, guilty or angry. A specific automatic thought can initiate a cluster of destructive thoughts, and for no apparent reason you can find yourself with a whole lot of negativity pounding in your head. This situation is common in sufferers of depression.

Realise that you learned these negative thoughts and they have become a habit of thinking destructively. They are not an unchangeable part of you and with a little effort they can be altered, even removed from your thinking.

Changing your automatic thoughts

At this stage you might be confused. You might be unsure if you'll find your automatic thoughts. It might seem too hard. Well, this is not the time to give up, to allow your usual negativity to suck you into a destructive thought pattern. Fight your negativity and read on. You'll find this a simple way of identifying the thoughts that give you all the trouble and a way of altering them. But be patient with yourself.

Step 1

Look at the types of automatic thoughts listed below that are common in many people. Perhaps you have some of the following thoughts as well:

- I'm useless.
- Nothing feels good or right any longer.
- I'm never going to get what I want.
- I'll always be a failure.
- How can i expect more of myself.
- It's too hard for me.
- Nobody cares about me.
- I'm a total loss.
- I wish i could be in another place.
- I'm a loser.
- I'm an idiot.

- Things will never change for me.
- I will never cope.
- I'm not smart enough.
- I don't look good.
- I'll never find friends.

Step 2

Think about your own destructive thoughts. You will identify them easily in negative feelings of hurt, worry, stress or fear. They may be in avoiding doing things, withdrawing, feeling angry, upset or in conflict with others.

Step 3

In a notebook draw up a table to list your own destructive thoughts throughout the day. This notebook ought to come along with you to school, your workplace or wherever you will be spending time that day. Try to list the actual thoughts, events or places that triggers your thinking. The following example shows you how you can record your thoughts.

**EXAMPLE OF A TYPICAL DAY'S DESTRUCTIVE
AUTOMATIC THOUGHTS**

SITUATION	DESTRUCTIVE THOUGHT
8.00 Grabbing breakfast on the run.	I can't face the day.
8.30 On the bus to work.	I won't manage work today.
8.45 Walking from the bus stop.	I won't cope.
9.15 At my desk.	It will be another day of endless mistakes.
9.20 In the toilet.	I can tell none of them like me.
9.45 At my desk.	I'm already making mistakes. I'm useless.
10.00 At my desk.	The boss will notice how useless I am.
10.45 At my desk.	I'll never manage to concentrate.
11.05 At my desk.	I don't know how I'll cope all day.
11.10 Coffee break.	No one talks to me or smiles at me.
11.30 At my desk.	I'm sure I'll mess up the report I'm typing.
11.45 Walking around the office.	They all ignore me.
12.00 In the lunch room.	I wish I could go home. I'm no use at all.
12.30 Walking back to my desk.	I'm sure that I'll mess up the report.
1.05 At my desk	More mistakes again. Stupid and useless.
2.15 My head is on the desk.	I can't get a thing right. I'm so tired.
3.00 Going to the toilet.	I'm sure that I'll lose this job.
3.40 Drinking coffee.	Maybe the coffee will make me concentrate.
4.00 A second cup of coffee.	What an idiot. The report is still not done.
4.35 At my desk.	The boss will think I'm incompetent.
5.00 Walking around the office.	They all ignore me.
5.45 In the bus home.	A horrible day. I didn't do a thing right.
6.00 Home.	I'm too tired to bother with food.
6.30 In bed.	All I want to do is sleep.

You will find that making these lists is worth all the trouble. If you listen into the way you think, you will find your destructive thoughts. Once you become aware of these thoughts, you will find that they lose their strength and their destructive power. BUT DO NOT TRY TO CHANGE THEM YET. In the following chapter you will learn how to change your destructive thoughts into more positive and constructive ones.

Grouping destructive automatic thoughts

You will notice in the above example that a number of "themes" or similar destructive patterns reoccur. Most people have a cluster of such thoughts that form part of their thinking. The number can vary from two to many more.

In the example you'll find these themes:

- Feeling useless or inadequate (stupid or making mistakes).
- Inability to concentrate.
- Tiredness and fear of not being able to make it through the day.
- Fear of not being liked.
- Lack of appetite.
- Feeling overwhelmed.

Discovering your own thinking themes gathered over a week will give you a clue as to your typical negative thoughts and make you more aware of them. Already you have taken the first step of changing your thinking. Now that you know about the way you think you will catch yourself being negative and the thoughts can no longer be automatic.

Healing story: *Learning to love*

Joseph clenched his fist in frustration and asked himself, *Why is God punishing me? What have I done to deserve this?* A tall, imposing man, he seemed old for his fifty-two years. He was the son of religious Jews brought up in an atmosphere of love and generosity. Depression ran in Joseph's family. His mother had suffered from it, his grandmother called it her quiet time, and an uncle had committed suicide. Joseph had experienced several bouts of depression, after episodes of severe stress in his childhood. His father who had been demanding and strict had beaten him often.

Recently a freeway was built that redirected the traffic. His once busy shop now stood on the old road and many of his customers were reluctant to travel though a choked intersection to reach it. Though his profits had dropped alarmingly he decided not to close down.

Daniel, his 17 year old son, played the clarinet and was set on studying music but Joseph tried to steer his son towards accountancy or law instead. "At least you'll have a stable profession, feed a family one day. After all you can play your clarinet as much as you like over the weekend." Daniel refused to even discuss his father's suggestion and the atmosphere between the two was tense.

The stress of his business troubles plus the lack of communication with his son had triggered a spell of depression. Joseph knew that he had to break through the wall between himself and Daniel but he did not know how. Too drained and negative, he avoided the problem.

One night a friend of Daniel's arrived at the house. Joseph usually sent all Daniel's friends straight up the stairs but this young man was a little older and hadn't been to the house before. He knocked on Daniel's bedroom door to tell him he had a visitor. As the door of his son's bedroom opened, he sniffed a pungent odour. Marijuana. He had smelled it on Daniel's clothing and hair recently and in his room. Joseph closed his son's door and said nothing.

Joseph avoided making a decision about selling his shop or closing it down and attempted to ignore the deadlock with Daniel. His son's marijuana smoking was another matter he refused to face. Instead Joseph turned to his past for comfort, focusing on his favourite memories of his mother and sister. Losing himself in daydreams, he chose to forget his parents were immigrants, his harsh father, the hard times they endured and the bullying he experienced at school. He longed to be in his childhood home. When his yearning became unbearable he drove to the suburb where they had once lived and searched for the house. He hadn't driven past it for several years and it was difficult to find. Initially, he was stunned that the semi-detached cottage had been painted pale apricot and its ornate gable, which he'd admired so much as a child, was dark green. After looking at it for a while he admitted to himself that the modern changes had made the house more attractive. *It's time to stop living in the past,* he told himself.

Friday nights, Joseph usually attended synagogue alone. Hoping to repair the rift between them, one Friday Daniel accompanied his father. Though they sat side by side, they barely spoke to each other. With his late father's torn prayer book in his hand, Joseph prayed for guidance. The cantor's singing and the mumble of prayer in the background led him to a deep place within himself and he asked himself again, why his son was smoking marijuana. He thought about the age gap between the two of them and acknowledged that there was much he didn't understand about his son. He certainly did not appreciate Daniel's musical talent. *Had he been wrong in trying to steer Daniel away from a career in music, his preference, and towards steadiness and practicality?* All he had achieved for his efforts was resentment. As Joseph recited the ancient prayers that were a part of his life, he became less aware of the sounds or the movements around him. What he noticed was that both he and Daniel were surrounded by a cocoon of light. He felt so close to Daniel right then. They were one, blended into a flickering, pulsating glow. Soon their comfort was interrupted by the clatter of the congregation standing. The service was over.

As they walked home again there was silence between them. When they neared the house Daniel spoke at last. "Dad, did you experience a weird sensation ... a warmth...a light?"

"Yes, indeed, the warmth of the Sabbath, a special gift to us." Joseph answered clumsily putting his arm around his son.

"I think you're right, Dad."

"We have a lot to talk about, Dan."

"Yeah, I guess we do."

"I don't know if you realise how much I love you and how important you are to me. I've been at fault, ignored your talent...been too self-absorbed and focused on my business."

Daniel nodded.

They were at the gate of their home when Joseph put his hand on his son's arm. "Dan, I have to tell you that I'm worried about you smoking marijuana. I haven't even told your mother...It would've upset her too much."

"Oh Dad, I don't smoke much. It helps me to unwind when I'm under pressure at school and it helps me to sleep at night. Anyway it's no big deal. All the kids in my class smoke it."

The following week they talked more easily as they walked to synagogue.

"Anyway, Dad I'm worried about you too. I can see you're not yourself. You look sad and tired most days."

"I know, I'm not feeling right...I'm sorry, I should have told you that I was depressed. I haven't done anything about it because I thought it would go away, like it has in the past."

They continued walking slowly. Both were deep in thought.

Joseph turned to Daniel "And I can tell you're not yourself either, Dan. What's upsetting you?"

"My music dad. I'm crazy about it, especially clarinet, and you've been against it. I think I've got the talent and that's what I want to do...to make it my career."

"I'm sorry, Dan. I should've realised and not tried to push you in another direction. All I wanted was the best for you." His voice faded.

"Yeah well ... let's forget it. The trouble is that I can't even play right now, I'm feeling too down. It looks like I've got the family depression bug. Maybe that's why I've been so uptight."

"When did it start?" Joseph asked, looking worried.

"There was a lot of pressure at school and anyway, the stuff we were learning didn't make any sense. I just wasn't coping, so I increased the amount of marijuana I was smoking to feel better but it hasn't worked."

Joseph sighed as they walked up the synagogue steps, "I had no idea you were feeling down too."

"Yeah, it's hit both of us and I guess we'll both have to do something about it."

Late that night Joseph and Estelle talked well into the night. This time Joseph told his wife the truth about himself and Daniel.

"We'll get help early next week. You both need to see a doctor. We have to tackle the depression first. Then we can attend to the other things – the shop, marijuana and Daniel's career," Estelle said calmly.

"You're right. I'll have some important business decisions to make that will free me up so that I can spend more time at home."

She nodded. "I'm sure the rest will start to fall into place."

TEN

IDENTIFYING UNREASONABLE BELIEFS

Your beliefs about yourself, others and the world around form the foundations of your thinking. Most of the time you may not even be aware that your beliefs govern your thinking and you don't question or challenge them. Many beliefs formed in childhood are strengthened or modified throughout your life. They allow you to make sense of your life and the events you experience. When depression strikes, destructive beliefs seem to swamp your thoughts.

2. UNREASONABLE BELIEFS

Unreasonable beliefs are the unrealistic beliefs and demands that often underlie automatic thinking. They can create a whole range of self-defeating emotions. They generate only one thing – trouble.

While a reasonable belief is real and factual, an unreasonable belief is neither true, real nor factual and can play havoc with your emotions. These destructive beliefs can worm their way into your everyday life, language and culture.

When you are depressed, unreasonable beliefs can intensify feelings of despair and hopelessness and seem to accentuate the need for unrealistic achievement, expectations or values that may seem out of your grasp. The following table illustrates some commonly held unreasonable beliefs.

COMMONLY HELD UNREASONABLE BELIEFS

DESTRUCTIVE BELIEFS	REASONABLE BELIEFS
I won't survive if I'm not loved	I'm a loveable person and I'm learning to accept myself. I don't need a partner to make me feel loved. I respect and care for myself. I am independent and can enjoy my life without a fixed relationship.
I must always do well. I can't handle the idea of failure.	It's OK to fail at things occasionally. I can learn from my mistakes. I realise that things don't always meet my expectations.
I won't cope if life doesn't go my way.	I'm beginning to cope better with my life. I'm slowly accepting that things don't always go smoothly, but if I take things slowly and don't expect too much of myself or others, I will manage most situations.
I deserve more out of life.	Most people have to work for what they have. If I start to work towards my goal there is no reason why I shouldn't achieve it. It serves no point being envious or resentful.
I shouldn't have to suffer	Life isn't easy for anyone but I'm getting stronger and should be able to cope better.
It's easier to avoid difficulties than to face them.	I don't need to hide or escape from others or myself. I am learning to face difficulties as I come across them.
I need to depend on someone stronger than myself.	It's fine to receive support but I'm becoming more independent.
It's not my fault that I'm so unhappy.	I am responsible for my life and the path I take. I can't blame my misfortunes on the past or on others.

3. DESTRUCTIVE THINKING STYLES

Of course, there are many more unreasonable beliefs than those listed. You'll be shocked to find how many there are in your thinking. But you will need to "listen in" carefully to catch them. Destructive thinking about yourself, your experience and the future allows your depression to thrive. Distortions occur in the form of negative, illogical reasoning and you may not be aware of them.

Authorities on cognitive behavioural therapy, Aaron T. Beck and Albert Ellis, identified many forms of distorted thinking common in depressed people. The following list is adapted from their various texts. Can you recognise a few in yourself?

The extremist

Extremists are rigid, all-or-nothing thinkers for whom things are either black or white. If you are unable to perform to your own high standards, you may become anxious, discrediting yourself for not being able to meet your high expectations. To attain second place in a race is unacceptable; winning is everything.

The sweeper

Sweepers think in generalisations so that if one attempt to achieve something doesn't work out then this implies that all future trials will automatically fail. For example, "I failed to get the job and it's just the beginning of a run of failures, so why bother looking for other jobs?"

The victim

Life seems to be governed by negative external forces. For example, "When I buy lottery tickets, I never have any luck like other people I know, who make a fortune. Something out there is always against me. I'll never be a winner."

The kangaroo

Kangaroos jump to negative conclusions without facts as back up. You imagine that you know what other people are thinking. Usually you assume they have negative thoughts about you. If you believe that you are disliked by a young man, you may think: "He's not meeting my gaze, and keeps looking away. I'm sure he doesn't want to talk to me. I always knew he didn't like me."

You may have the habit of anticipating how badly things will turn out in the future, certain that your dire predictions will come to pass.

The exaggerator

Exaggerators blow negative things out of proportion. A typical exaggerated thought may be: "I totally destroyed that food processor, I'm always messing things up. What a clumsy idiot I am! No one will ever be able to fix it. How awful. How terrible. It's a disaster!"

The wizard

Wizards imagine that the way they feel can cause or alter things around them. They believe in negative powers, and in the way emotions magically seem to reflect the truth or cause awful things to happen to themselves or others. This is an example of wizardry: "I argued with my daughter this morning before she left for school and she was so upset that she slipped and hurt her knee. I must have caused her fall. It's all my fault. I should be more careful about what I say. I'm a dangerous person, always causing trouble."

The moraliser

The moraliser tortures himself with demanding and moralising statements, such as "I should", "I ought to", "I must", and you feel guilty if you don't meet these demands. Other people seem to let you down continually by not living and behaving in the way you would like.

The labeller

Labellers use mistakes or failures to confirm their negative view of themselves, such as, "Well, what can one expect from an idiot like me, and I'm not surprised I lost the game, I'm totally useless at cards and always have been. I'm a card fool and not much good at other things either!"

Assess your destructive thinking style

Depression can cause a destructive way of looking at the world, and unproductive ways of thinking feeds its fire, so that it can filter into every aspect of your life, robbing you of confidence and hope for the future. Make a note of your own typical thinking style. This will help you to break the habit of negative thinking. Sometimes thinking can be a mixture of two or more styles.

If a pattern of negativity emerges in your own thinking, view it rationally. This will help you to understand those self-defeating patterns that sustain your depression. You will gradually change them. It's natural to feel despondent at the work ahead in making these changes, but it will have been worth the effort when you are no longer weighed down with negativity. If you persevere, each day you'll challenge more and more of the irrational patterns that govern your thinking and soon you'll notice improvements in your self-esteem and optimism.

Healing story: *The Wheel of Fortune*

Dave relished his highs. He didn't know when he would spiral down again. He was unpredictable and unreliable at work, irritable and changeable at home. His moods threw his life into disarray and upset many people. He dismissed his erratic behaviour as a phase that would eventually pass. Though he toyed with the idea of seeking medical advice, he talked himself out of it. His latest spell of elation had lasted two weeks so far and he intended to enjoy it with frequent visits to his favourite gambling spot, the casino.

As he swaggered into the casino, he slicked back his hair and smiled confidently. He was feeling on top of things and was prepared to gamble on almost anything – games, horses, dogs, football, cards or lotteries. Grinning, he viewed the plush interior and grabbed a drink from a waitress. The pulsating pace invaded his senses and he could hardly wait to have a go. "I can feel it in my bones," he said to himself. "Today is going to be my lucky day. I won't hold back, I'll give it my all."

The dazzling casino cave with its lights flickering hypnotically intrigued him. As he sipped his drink, he eyed the attractive, scantily dressed women. The rows of clinking slot machines beckoned. He tried his luck on one and won a few dollars. A win, with a cascade of coins tinkling through the machine, was a thrill and cause to celebrate with a double whisky.

Roulette was his favourite game. The spinning wheel thrilled him, and with a stir of almost childish delight he spread several chips around the table. As the tiny ball stopped at his number, adrenaline rushed through his body with such power that it was hard to contain his urge to shout with joy. He piled up his winnings, celebrated with another double and moved on. A patrolling muscle man watched him suspiciously.

I knew I'd win. I've got to keep going with my lucky streak, he said to himself, as he moved on to the blackjack tables that filled the centre aisle. The dealers in their neat, maroon uniforms stood poised for action. *Come on, come on 21.* He rubbed his hands together in anticipation.

After several games he had lost all that he had won. The group of gamblers around the table looked up momentarily and then went on with their own quest. With his mind racing and his head throbbing, he worked his way down the black grotto, crammed with tables and gamblers, towards the Wheel of Fortune. He liked the name and felt so certain that his numbers would come up that impulsively he put down a huge sum of money, hoping for a killing.

The lights danced while he lost and lost again. He had been drinking heavily and felt unsteady. Flopping into a chair, he wiped his flushed face with his handkerchief. The gloss of his high mood was wearing off and the downward slide had begun. As the wheel spun and the fairy lights beckoned to him, a mixture of tiredness and alcohol overwhelmed him. He felt floaty, a sensation of being present and yet far away at the same time.

Then his blurred vision sharpened. As clearer forms zoomed in, he found himself in a functional, stainless steel gambling hall. The dark, voluptuous, cocoon with its myriad of fairy lights disappeared. The roulette and blackjack tables were made of practical steel. At least the clink of gambling machines and the sound of a win with an avalanche of coins surging through the machine had not changed. There were fewer croupiers and most of the games took place on large colourful computer screens. There were no cashiers as computers took care of all dealings. He looked round at the gamblers dressed in similar clothing and shrugged.

He moved to the wheel of fortune, picked up a few chips and threw them down. *Heavens, this place is boring.*

A tall man next to him must've noticed his dissatisfaction and commented, "This is 2030, and we're proud of our changes from the decadence at the turn of the century...your time, judging by your clothes."

"We're in 2030?" Dave repeated, stunned. "At least people haven't given up gambling, I'm pleased about that."

"There are even more gamblers than ever," the man said. "The government has tried to get rid of drugs and gambling, but it's a waste of time." He touched Dave's arm. "Come, I'll show you what's happened to your world."

Dave followed him out of the main exit and into the streets lined with shacks. He gasped at the beggars on the pavements and the ground strewn with syringes.

"They make up about an eighth of the population...fed by the state and given free medical treatment but it hasn't helped." He sighed. "Look at them! We've conquered all the old diseases like cancer and AIDS, made progress with heart conditions using genetic engineering and nuclear medicine, but these people are our shame. If it wasn't for my wife pulling me away from drugs a few years ago, I'd be one too. I'm still an addict, can't stop gambling."

Dave and his new friend left the ugliness of the streets and returned to the metallic casino.

Later, the tinkle of glass and the loud applause accompanying a winning spin carried Dave back into the cave with its flickering lights. He looked around to assure himself that he really was back in the year 2013, and sighed with relief. The wheel whizzed and he continued to play half -heartedly with the few chips in his hand. His peek at the future had distressed him and his mood tumbled. There were no clocks in the casino and he cursed himself for purposely leaving his watch at home. Picking up his remaining chips he stumbled towards the cash desk.

"Easy now...it's about time for you to go home," said a powerfully built man as he steered Dave towards the exit. "I'll call you a cab."

Dave didn't reply but seethed with anger. *How dare that upstart try to push me about.*

By the time the taxi arrived, the fresh night air had roused him. He shrank back into the seat. *Chucked out of the casino by a bouncer ... an all-time low.*

The low mood that had begun its course in the casino continued for several weeks. The large amount of alcohol he consumed dragged him further down.

"Yeah, yeah," he answered his wife who suggested he seek help. Always the gambler, he took a coin out of his pocket. *Heads I go to the doctor tomorrow, tails I don't.* He tossed the coin into the air and it landed on tails. *Oh well, I'll see how I go over the next few months.*

ELEVEN

MAKING CHANGES TO DESTRUCTIVE THOUGHTS

If a pattern of negativity has emerged in your thinking, viewing it rationally will help you to understand the self-defeating patterns that sustain your depression. This will enable you to distance yourself and gradually make changes. There are several ways of altering your thinking and you can experiment with the following approaches or combinations.

Methods of altering your thoughts

1. Clarifying and altering your destructive thoughts.

2. Assessing your thinking.

3. Thought challenging.

4. Weighing up the advantages and disadvantages.

5. Thought stopping.

6. Making affirmations.

7. Journal writing.

1. CLARIFYING AND ALTERING YOUR DESTRUCTIVE THOUGHTS

This rational method will increase your awareness of destructive thinking. It may seem to be a complicated or lengthy technique but the time spent on it will be worthwhile. By using this method you will examine your thoughts critically. You will understand more about the situations in which your thoughts occur and the way in which they affect you physically and emotionally. It may also help you to improve the despondent mood that accompanies depression. Once you have worked through this process, I hope that it will seem logical to change your negative thoughts.

In the following example the thought *I'll never make new friends,* is used first.

The situation where the thought occurs is at work, where it creates feelings of anxiety and loneliness. Emotional and physical reactions to the thought are anxiety with fast breathing and palpitations. When the thought is changed to an alternative and more constructive one, the distressed emotions calm down, and apart from a few palpitations, the physical reaction stops. Other faulty thoughts are then examined in the same manner.

CLARIFYING AND ALTERING YOUR DESTRUCTIVE THOUGHTS

Thought	Situation	Emotion	Physical reaction	Constructive thought	Result
I'll never make new friends.	At work.	Anxious, lonely and unwanted.	Palpitations Fast breathing.	There is absolutely no evidence to support the idea that I won't make new friends. I will try to be more sociable.	Feel calmer. Palpitations have settled down. Breathing normally.
I'm sure I'll make a fool of myself.	Learning a difficult new task.	Anxious. Feeling flat.	Fast breathing Sweaty.	I haven't made a fool of myself before, so there is no reason to fear that I will this time. Doing well at things is desirable, but not the most important thing in life. I will try my best.	More relaxed My body is calming down.

If he can't understand how I feel I will be very upset.	Out with a friend.	Anxious or depressed.	Palpitations Hot and cold sensations.	It would be nice if he understood how I feel. I will try to explain but if he still doesn't understand I'll be a bit disappointed but it's not the end of the world. My mood is not dependent on his understanding.	Calmer and not upset or anxious.

2. ASSESSING YOUR THINKING

Start by making lists of your destructive and unreasonable thoughts. Then review each one and decide whether the thoughts have a logical foundation by asking yourself the following questions and decide to accept or reject them:

- Is this a reasonable and realistic thought?
- Is this thought factual?
- Is there any evidence that it is true?
- Could I look at it another way?
- Is it an important thought and will it be important in a few months?
- What advice would I give someone else (concerning this thought in this situation)?
- What would someone else think about it?
- Is my reaction in proportion to the actual event?
- Is there a more balanced way of looking at it?

3. THOUGHT CHALLENGING

The following table illustrates how to challenge your thoughts objectively by writing them down.

THOUGHT CHALLENGING

The destructive thought: **Nobody cares about me.** *Challenging the thought:* *Ask yourself*: Is this a reasonable and realistic thought? Is there any evidence to support this thought? *Now challenge the thought:* NO it is not a reasonable thought!
Although it seems as if nobody cares, I am aware that many people are concerned about me. Anyway I'm not dependent on what other people think of me. *Is there any proof to support this thought?* NO. There is no proof at all. It is a destructive thought. *Is there a more balanced way of looking at it?* YES. I know it is my depression talking. I might feel quite different in a few weeks. *Does the thought add to my positive feelings about myself?* NO. It is an unpleasant thought that adds nothing to my wellbeing. *My decision* Do I want to hold on to this thought or let it go? NO. I don't want to keep the thought. It is totally destructive. **Changed thought** Some people do care about me.

4. WEIGHING UP THE ADVANTAGES AND DISADVANTAGES

This is a well-known method of clarifying thoughts or making decisions.

In the following table this thought is assessed: I want to go to a concert tonight but I feel guilty. It is a waste of time and I should be studying.

WEIGHING UP ADVANTAGES AND DISADVANTAGES

ADVANTAGES	DISADVANTAGES
The singer is my favourite performer and I want to go to the concert.	The venue is far away and I'll have to get a lift from John. But John drinks too much and I'm afraid of going in the car with him.
The huge venue is wonderful and I will enjoy the excitement.	The venue is too big and I may not hear very well. Crowds create excitement but sometimes they spoil concerts.
It would be a break from study. I haven't been out for a long time.	I'm behind with my work and I need to catch up.
I will experience it and not have to watch it on TV.	TV will have a clearer version I will see it easily and comfortably.
I will be able to catch up easily with my studies.	If I go I'll be tired by the next day and lose valuable study time.

My decision: I would rather be safe and not waste time. I will have a clearer view if I watch the concert on television.

5.   THOUGHT STOPPING

Stopping a thought takes patience but is an extremely useful technique for controlling negative thoughts. It can be used alone or in conjunction with the other strategies for controlling destructive thoughts. Each time you are aware of thinking a destructive thought follow one of these actions:

1.   Snap your fingers...and tell yourself to STOP and replace the destructive thought with a constructive one.

2.   As well as telling yourself to STOP, imagine a traffic stop sign every time you think negatively.

6.   MAKING AFFIRMATIONS

An affirmation is a positive statement in the first person and present tense describing yourself in the most desirable way. It is another method of counteracting your negative thoughts. To be effective, affirmations should be brief, simply worded, and repeated regularly to create a clear picture of yourself achieving your goal. Affirmations can play an important role in your recovery, by helping to remind you of your positive qualities and the path you have chosen to follow. These are some examples of useful affirmations:

- I appreciate my skills and capabilities.
- I am feeling better every day.
- I will start slowly and progress.
- I am loved and valued by my family.
- Each day I gain more and more insight into my problems.
- I accept the person I am.
- Communication in my relationships is improving.
- I am happy with my weight and my general appearance.
- I am a lovable person.

Practise creating a few of your own affirmations that describe yourself and your life in an ideal way. You can be as imaginative as you like when painting the picture you would like to see of yourself. Once you have written your affirmations, place copies of them strategically on your bedroom mirror, on the fridge or on the bathroom wall. Repeat them on waking and before sleep, during the day at any time or during relaxation.

7. JOURNAL WRITING

This is one of the easy and most effective ways of healing your depression. In writing a journal you will be able to explore your emotions and find ways of coping that will help you on your healing path. When you are depressed you may feel despondent and towards the end of the day worrying thoughts may dominate your thinking and interfere with your sleep. Interrupt your thoughts with a reality check. One of the ways of doing this successfully is by writing your thoughts down in a journal.

Suggestions for writing your personal journal

- Put aside 5 –10 minutes a day to write your journal.

- Write your journal entry at about the same time every day. You might chose to write in the morning to express all your worries, fears and expectations before you face the day or at a point of closure in the day for reflection and express any concerns you have for that night. Before leaving work, or after your evening meal is a good time too.

- Don't work on your journal immediately before going to sleep as your mind may become too active and you may have difficulty falling asleep.

- Try to forget about grammar or spelling as you write. Just express everything that is in your mind.

- Be open and honest with yourself. If there is personal material in your journal that you don't want others to read find a hiding place.

- Journal writing should not be a task or a chore. It will be of no value unless you view it as an opportunity to develop as a person and learn more about yourself each day.

- It is also a means of finding creative strategies for coping, so make notes of how you could best use your ideas.

The following example is a guide to help you to control faulty thoughts that build up during the day. These are some of the categories you might want to include.

DAILY JOURNAL CATEGORIES

1. The pleasant or worthwhile experiences I had today
They are not necessarily important or essential events. They could include taking a walk, chatting to a friend, looking in shop windows, enjoying looking at flowers in the park, sitting in the sun.

2. Things that worry me that I can't control
All those things that worry you, that you can do nothing about, such as waiting to hear from the bank about a loan, concern about paying taxes, having to work according to the rules of a company or institution, issues other people decide for you or upsetting things someone said to you.

3. Ways to change things that bother me
Some worries can be turned around, for example, fear of having made an error at work. This could keep you awake at night but speaking to your supervisor about your concerns will clarify the situation. You might be concerned about an argument with an old friend. If you phone your friend and discuss the issues you disagreed about, the unpleasantness is likely to clear up.

4. My plans for tomorrow
This includes items such as plans for work, study, exercise, leisure, social activities.

5. The little extra things I need to remember
This category is about personal things that need doing, such as picking up the dry cleaning, buying stamps, phone calls you need to make, remembering a friend's birthday.

6. My affirmation for tomorrow
This is a positive inspirational statement in the first person. For example, I am a loving person. I am gradually getting better.

7. Feelings I need to express
You might have feelings that need expression. These might be feelings that bother you about your illness or other matters, such as worries about medication, the pace of your recovery, the recurrence of flat moods.

8. Any other comment
This refers to anything important you are thinking or feeling or any notes you want to make.

AN EXAMPLE OF A JOURNAL PAGE

1.The pleasant experiences I had today
Went to the beach. Enjoyed the sunshine. Found an unusual shell. Had a short walk

2.Things that worry me that I can't control
That my new tablets might have side-effects What my ex colleagues think of me Whether I qualify for a special pension My tax bill

3. Ways to change things that bother me
Speak to my doctor about the side-effects of the tablets Find out about qualifications for a special pension.

4. Plans for tomorrow
Go to the supermarket Lunch with a friend Make a doctor's appointment

5. Little things I need to remember
Buy sunscreen Look for a suitable hat Buy dog food

6. My affirmation for tomorrow
I feel healthier each day

7. Feelings I need to express
Sad feelings about my past – anger and resentment about the times I was bullied at school. I must discuss this with my counsellor.

8. Any other comment
Met a friend today. Hope I see her tomorrow.

Later that day or the next day

If the same things you noted in your journal earlier in the day, continue to concern you or nag, tell yourself that you have already written them down and that they are taken care of…that you will think about them later when you write up your journal again. But, if new thoughts intrude or worry you, scribble them down quickly and tell yourself that you will include them in your journal later in the day. The concept of this type of journal is to help you discipline and structure your thinking. It also limits the number of your troublesome thoughts each day.

You now have several strategies to use to break down your destructive thoughts. Read all the suggested techniques in this chapter and experiment with each one until you find the method that works best for you. Even small alterations in the way you think and feel will make the work of doing these exercises worthwhile. Any of these methods mentioned in this chapter or a combination of them are extremely effective in changing your thinking.

As changing your thoughts is the key to a new way of approaching your thinking and feeling to heal your depression, do not move on to the next step until you have worked with this process. Do not be distressed if you go through a phase where you find yourself stopping a thought but not yet being able to replace it with a constructive one. This is a natural transition phase and soon you will master constructive thinking and feel the better for it.

Turning your depression around will take patience as well as perseverance. You may be dissatisfied with your efforts if shifts in the way you feel are gradual rather than dramatic. Realise that you may be expecting too much of yourself too soon and that you are likely to see small or subtle changes before you notice the major ones. Try not to place time limits on your improvement, as the pressure generated will add to your discomfort. Experiment with several of the techniques mentioned till you find the strategies that work for you. Your goal is to change thoughts that pull you down and worsen your depression. Don't give up, keep working at those changes until you feel more optimistic and positive.

Healing story: *The Lake*

Lake Taupo is so vast that its stretch of blue disappears into the sky. I had been travelling in New Zealand and was told not to miss a visit. There were many stories of its mystical qualities so I had to see it for myself. The lake lay in a crater of an inactive volcano. There were bubbling thermal mud pools and icy spots. I tried to swim in it but gave it up. The water felt heavy and had a strange mineral smell.

One afternoon I took a cruise on what must've been a replica of an old steamboat. Sailing with the breeze on the water was a welcome escape from the hot day. The passengers were a mix of people, who like myself seemed to have nothing much to do.

"The Maoris are a Polynesian people and have been on this land for about seven hundred years after their many travels from South East Asia," I heard the guide say, before the motion of the boat sent me to sleep. When I woke we were almost in the middle of the lake, the old boat sidling up to tall rocks covered in Maori carvings that formed a natural entrance. An enormous warlike mask was heavily carved on the nearest slab of rock and on the surrounding area were animals from Maori legends and culture. The mask both frightened and repulsed me and I was certain that it was a definite 'keep out' sign to all strangers of the known and the spirit world. I felt sure that the face seemed to guard not only the lake but the mountain behind it as well.

"Strange things can happen on these waters," the guide said without further explanation.

A few sceptical murmurs came from the passengers. "Oh yeah, tell us. We'd like to here all about it."

"You don't believe me," he said with a shrug and stared out towards the horizon for several minutes before he spoke again. "I'll tell you what happened to me about ten years ago and you can judge it yourselves."

I sat up against the wooden seat and waited.

"About ten years ago I was going through a terrible time. I'd split up with my wife and was living alone. I was so shaken up that I couldn't even sail my boat. I suppose I got used to being alone after a time and one afternoon I felt like sailing again. As I was heading home and the sun was dipping down, I saw it in the distance...a canoe manned by Maori warriors moving like a fast machine. Then, as they came from nowhere they disappeared."

A roar of comments came from the passengers. The guide held up his hand to still them. At the time I wondered why he was telling us this story and if he told the same one to every load of passengers he ferried around the lake.

"Please, let me finish the story. It's a special one...and I only tell it occasionally." I nodded to myself cynically.

He glanced at us, straightened his shoulders and continued. "The word goes that a Maori chief once saw a canoe on the lake just before a massive volcano blew its top and destroyed villages around this area. People round here say he thought it was a sign of coming disaster...and he was right." He lit a cigarette and took a draw. "You can't know how scared I was of what I'd seen that day. I was back to the harbour in no time asking if anyone else had seen the canoe but none of the sailors had.

"I forgot about the canoe until one Sunday about six months later. It was a stormy day and I was trying to stay afloat in churned up waters near the deepest part of the lake when I saw the canoe again. It was closer to me this time and the carved red wood and all the oarsmen were clear. There must've been a dozen men with bare chests, wearing grass skirts and their bodies and faces were covered with tattoos. In spite of the waves that day, rowing together they swept through that water like one man. Well, it was something to see. I tried to keep my eyes on the canoe but part of the time it disappeared into the wild waters and sunshine. It rode towards the shore and then onto the dark sand of the lake beach. The men climbed out and their women folk and children ran to greet them. They hugged and kissed and raced up the beach together. Then the pictured faded."

"Weird," a man behind me said.

"I tried following them but they'd gone. The beach was empty."

"So what did you make of it," I called out to the guide impatiently. He held up his hand to stop me and the others questioning him.

"All I can say is that it made a change to my life," he said, steering the steamship into its berth."

I shook my head, puzzled by the unsatisfactory ending to his story. Our trip was over and a queue waited for the next tour. We filed off the boat while he busied himself with the new crop of passengers.

After my stay at Taupo, I returned to Auckland and flew home to find that my girlfriend had moved out of the house. I can't say I was surprised as we hadn't been getting along for months. Being alone in the house unsettled me. I couldn't understand it. I had enjoyed travelling alone for almost a month. I flung myself into work and was soon almost as tired as I had been before the holiday. In spite of my efforts, I missed out on a promotion to someone with better qualifications. The disappointment knocked me about. I knew I had to move on but where? The uncertainty and thought of change made me jumpy.

Weeks later I saw a poster in the city advertising Maori singing and dancing. The image of that masked head guarding the watery wall came back to me as clearly as the day I'd seen it.

That night, over a cold beer or two, I thought about the guide's story. What it had meant to the guide wasn't important, nor whether it was true or not. That it was back in my thoughts, told me that it had to be important to me. Weeks later, I'd given up trying to understand myself or the story's special meaning, when it hit me like a thunder bolt. I was feeling alone and panicky at the time. I was obsessed about a job that wasn't offering me enough and I had cut myself off from everyone close to me – my parents, relatives, old school friends and work mates. I had missed the danger signs and the nervous roar inside me warned that it could get worse. I needed to be one of a team rowing with others and welcomed home. At last, I understood. It was my aloneness that was causing the anxiety. That was it!

Though it's not easy, I'm trying my best to sort things out. I took the plunge and answered a few job advertisements in the newspaper. I've contacted one or two old friends and I'll be having lunch with mum and dad this Sunday. As long as I take it slowly, I'll get myself going.

TWELVE

STRENGTHENING MOTIVATION

Depression can drain your desire to do things. Many of your former activities may no longer interest you and people you once spent time with, you now withdraw from.

Your energy levels might be so low that you feel unable to tackle basic tasks, such as washing clothes, cleaning the house, answering phone messages or paying bills. Being aware of a pile of tasks waiting to be done can result in guilty or negative feelings about yourself.

Depression can be a self-defeating cycle. The less you do the less you want to do. If you begin to believe that you are useless and worthless, you may no longer even try, feeling that there's no point. The longer you ponder over all the things you ought to be doing but cannot, and the expectations of others that you cannot fulfil, the worse you feel. Self-defeating thoughts occur because you've allowed your negative thoughts to dominate your thinking.

What can you do about apathy, lethargy and procrastination?

Be kind to yourself

Try not to expect too much of yourself. Be realistic, if you are depressed, it will take you longer than before to do things and do them well. You may make mistakes but don't be angry with yourself. Try to be patient, it will take you a while to recover.

Try not to shut out loved ones and friends

Though you would like to shut the door and be alone, force yourself to allow your loved ones into your life. Discuss how you feel with them and allow them to help you. Being with others will give you the support you need to get going.

The value of structure and routine

Most people feel better with a routine or a schedule. Work out a daily schedule and try your best to stick to it. Even go as far as setting up a time table with periods of work and relaxation. Even small tasks act as a distraction. If you only accomplish part of what you intend to do, it will boost your confidence

Where possible eat at the same time each day, rest at the same time and try to fit activities into time slots that are comfortable and predictable. This will help at first to set up a pattern that returns you to good health.

These are some of the activities that could become routine and aid your recovery:

- Set an alarm. An alarm ringing may not only be a signal to get out of bed. You might set an alarm to remind yourself to exercise, take your medication or make a meal. The ringing alarm serves as a reminder and helps to organise your day.

- Try to dress every day. If you get into the habit of getting dressed in comfortable clothes you will be setting the base for other activities to follow like meeting a friend, cleaning, walking or exercising.

- Go outside at least once a day. Taking a few deep breaths of fresh air and take a brief walk might be a start.

Care for yourself

Eat nourishing food, even if you no longer eat as much as previously. Eat healthy snacks between meals to boost your energy when you need it. Have sufficient rest. If you are depressed, this is the time you need to take extra care of yourself. Tiredness is a common symptom of depression and sound sleep is not always possible. Reverse your tiredness by taking a short nap.

Small steps

Once you have begun to function within a routine, set up small simple goals and tackle one project or idea at a time. This is not a time to take on too much and risk sliding backwards. Work slowly at achieving the most important goal of recovery and enjoying your life again.

How to motivate a depressed loved one

Listen

Attend to what the depressed person has to say and help him to feel at ease about discussing his fears and concerns. Talking to an open-minded caring person will often bring a great deal of relief and feelings of being supported.

Acknowledge the problem

Having an outside person acknowledge his suffering may lighten his load. He may feel guilty about no longer being able to perform tasks or work and consider himself lazy. Many depressed people don't even know that they have a medical condition or what it is called. Helping him to understand his condition and the need to seek professional help is an important first step. Helping him to find appropriate help is the next step.

Cook healthy meals

Depressed people often have very little appetite. It is therefore very important to make certain that the little they eat is appetizing and nourishing. A well-balanced meal with all the proteins and other nutrients is essential. Information about food that may help depression is available elsewhere in the book.

Encourage activity

If at all possible encourage the depressed person to leave the house and spend at least a short while outdoors. Some joint activity like walking would be helpful. Even sitting out in the sun for while is a good idea. The sharing of time together will demonstrate your genuine concern. Suggestions that the depressed person might take up former hobbies or new interests with your help would do a great deal towards improving chances of his recovery.

Healing story: *Search for Meaning*

Each day Ravi examined his face for tell-tale ageing lines. From the day he turned forty, youth was almost an obsession. He dieted, jogged daily and took large doses of vitamins to maintain his health and appearance. The top city barber styled his hair and he wore expensive clothing.

During the past year he had felt increasingly lethargic. Even his job as a clerk of the court had become boring when previously it had been a challenge. As an escape, he threw himself into social engagements. At the end of each evening out he was faced with dull emptiness. Though he bought a fast car, his initial pleasure of exceeding the speed limit didn't last.

Later, in a search for answers, he visited his swami but left half-way through the discussion. He then consulted a Hindu sage and a clairvoyant but his quest drew no satisfying answers. After many months, he decided to visit India, the land of his birth.

Within a few weeks he left with a pair of sturdy boots, jeans, tee shirts and a bedroll. He landed in Delhi, where he was confronted with the mass of people, noise, traffic congestion and overwhelming poverty he had forgotten. There were several spiritually significant sites he wanted to visit. He joined a tour to the Taj Mahal but its grace and haunting beauty didn't stir him as it would have years before. After none of the ancient temples proved inspiring, he flew on to Varanasi, the pilgrimage centre along the banks of the sacred Ganges River. Holy men smeared with mud and ash appeared odd and their years of ritual self-sacrifice and discipline through all seasons and weather, were hard to understand. Many, like him, had found their business or personal lives worthless or empty and were on a quest for spiritual enlightenment. He passed the funeral pyres that carried those who had been cremated on their final journey down the sacred river. At the river's steps, he observed pilgrims dressed in white bathing in the filthy and polluted waters, and left hurriedly.

At the tea estates in Darjeeling he hoped to find the estate where he had lived as a youth. The breathtaking views of the plantations with the mountain range in the background brought a lump to his throat but the rambling, family house had been replaced by new, modern apartments.

He combed the area for relatives and friends, but found they had moved on.

It was while staring at the mountains he at last realised that it was his flat mood that had made every temple, and landmark he visited seem uninteresting. Aware that in his present mood he would not connect with the spirituality of India and find the answers he sought, he returned home.

A few weeks after his return, he learnt that his cousin Jay was hospitalised with terminal cancer. They had played together as children and a bond existed between them, even though as adults they rarely saw each other. Armed with fruit and flowers, he visited his cousin in hospital. Jay was hooked up to a drip and was receiving oxygen, his ravaged body shrunken and his face pale.

Each night after work Ravi was at his cousin's bedside. Though he tried to lift Jay's spirits with recounts of his visit to India, his cousin turned away. Ravi tried reading to him or tempting his meagre appetite with delicacies. As Jay's illness progressed, Ravi felt closer to his cousin than ever. After Jay died, Ravi felt the loss intensely.

Weeks later he was thinking about Jay, when he realised that it was the first time since childhood that he had genuinely given of himself. He knew now that his visit to India had provided none of the answers he'd sought as he'd been closed to the experience. His brief grasp of a loving relationship with Jay had shown him a different perspective.

Ravi no longer yearned for a youthful image. He followed a more moderate regime of exercise and diet and his days became more serene and predictable.

THIRTEEN

SETTING GOALS

The most important goals you need to consider are those concerning your recovery. Structuring each day will help you to beat depression more quickly. So, when you set yourself goals, always bear in mind that each day's struggle to achieve your planned activities is worthwhile. Congratulate yourself if you have met your goal and try to stretch yourself a little further in the next few days.

Plan your activities

If you are depressed, attempting to focus on tasks for the day may seem impossible. But, having plans, no matter how small or short-term does speed up your recovery. Focusing on a task will distract you from your troubles for a while and achieving what you set out to do will boost your confidence. Try to follow these suggestions:

- Start by planning simple, short activities of up to one hour, a day ahead at a time. Do your planning the night before for the following day.

- Only plan for one day at a time.

- Set up a time table and select no more than three activities.

- While you follow your plan, try to return to your routine of getting up, eating and sleeping.

- If possible choose doing things you once enjoyed.

- If you miss your activity don't worry. Try to achieve the next one.

- Write down each activity you attempt and note your pleasure or lack of it. Also note whether the task you set yourself was achieved or not.

Try this simple approach for about a week. If you find you are struggling to do as much as you would like, try to complete only one task a day but choose one that gives you pleasure. Only build up the number of hours you tackle when you feel comfortable.

Case study

When Gavin became depressed, he hung around the house feeling guilty. The dirty plates were piling up in the kitchen and the lawn was overgrown. He hadn't been to see his mother for two weeks. Previously he visited her twice a week at least.

He muttered to himself often about his worthlessness. In his head he heard his father telling him what a "lazy, useless idiot" he was. Each day he made promises to himself that he would do everything he needed to tackle, but by midday he hadn't even begun, and the rest of the day faded with nothing done.

It was a new counsellor who convinced him that he could become more active. She helped him to form some simple plans. By the next week, he visited his mother and shortly after that he began to clean the kitchen, but he did not make a good job of it. He enjoyed swimming and walking so he added them to his list.

Within a few weeks he managed to achieve his planned activities until he became too ambitious and tried to spend longer periods on each activity and do more. When heavy rain stopped him swimming and walking, he tried to replace the activities with others but failed. As a result he sank into a negative spell of self-blame. *You shouldn't have even started this, you knew you'd muck it up*, he told himself.

Much later with the help of his counsellor he stuck to simple plans. He tried to stop beating up on himself and was more successful.

If you are not achieving your goal

Perhaps you are not enjoying the activity. It could be too complicated or you are expecting too much of yourself. There might have been reasons beyond your control that prevented you from achieving your aims. If reducing the time spent and number of activities attempted doesn't help, don't give up. Try another approach. Learning to be more flexible is one of the ways you will beat depression.

Break down the activity

Break an activity down into small steps. Instead of tackling the entire activity, approach it step by step. As each step is achieved move on to the next one until the task is completed.

Gavin's plan to clean the kitchen could be broken down into the following steps:

1. Go into the kitchen and decide what needs to be done.

2. Pile up the dirty plates and cutlery in the sink.

3. Collect all the pots and dirty dishes littering the kitchen.

4. Clean the bench tops and sink.

5. Put detergent into the sink and begin to wash the cutlery and dishes.

6. Place them on a draining board.

7. Dry them and put them away.

8. Scrub and clean one pot at a time.

9. Put the pots away.

10. Mop the floor.

A planning table

As you achieve more and more, move on to longer term plans for a day or two ahead. Then extend the time until you can comfortably plan for a week ahead.

A longer-term goal that can be achieved in about six to eight weeks, is usually more complex, such as inviting a friend to your home for a meal, booking for a play or sporting activity in advance. If you manage to achieve the last goal comfortably, you are ready for something more challenging, such as a long weekend away, planned three weeks in advance. After accomplishing this, you will realise that you are coping well and you may want to set some even longer-term goals.

- Always start with the most pleasurable activity.

- Establish the steps you need to take to reach your objective. Having an aim is insufficient – you need to know how to get there.

- In those early stages of planning, your goals need to be clear, simple and specific. Clearly outline the tasks and the amount of time to be spent on achieving them, such as a 30-minute walk, washing the dog or cleaning two rooms in the house.

- If you push yourself to achieve beyond your area of comfort, realise that you may feel anxious. Though a slight degree of anxiety can be a healthy challenge, too much anxiety may cause you to abandon your objective.

- In these early stages, *do not* attempt tasks that draw you into areas where you feel intensely vulnerable or extremely insecure.

- When you reach some or all of your goals, reward yourself with something small that pleases you: special bath oil, an inexpensive cosmetic, listening to your favourite music or a chocolate.

Difficulties in achieving your goal

If you are physically ill

If you are ill and need to stay in bed or stay indoors, do not push yourself to do more. Your activity can be in keeping your mind busy by watching interesting programmes on TV, reading or doing simple crafts. Later when your doctor allows you to do more you can increase your activity levels.

If you have setbacks

If you are finding difficulty in achieving all or part of the goal you have set yourself, be gentle with yourself and review your goal-setting methods. Were you aiming too high or expecting too much of yourself in too short a time? Have another look at your priorities. You may need to make adjustments. Have you listed the necessary steps? You might have missed some. Perhaps you weren't feeling well enough to tackle your particular goal, or maybe lack of motivation took its toll.

Don't give up if this seems too hard a task. Wait a week or two and start work on simpler or shorter-term goals until you are more confident at it. Remember that recovering from your depression is your primary aim.

Healing story: *Trapped*

Jason shivered as he looked beyond the bars of his cell onto a bleak, icy day. The concrete of the yard was covered in soupy sleet and the exercise deprived prisoners could not venture out. He was as miserable as the weather and nothing could shift his mood.

He and a friend had robbed a bank and were serving a two year prison sentence. With a year already behind him, he faced one more Christmas inside. Though no one had been threatened or hurt in the robbery and most of the money had been returned, he was ashamed that greed had influenced him to do something so despicable. Every day during the exercise break he could be seen pacing in the yard.

Initially Jason coped with prison life. He was a good listener and had a sense of humour which made him popular with the guards and his fellow prisoners. But no matter how hard he tried to laugh it off or pretend that all was well, the confined space, endless routine and severe discipline wore away his resilience. He stopped chatting to other prisoners and telling jokes. At twilight, he sat in his grey cell with nothing but another sleepless night ahead.

One wintery afternoon, the prison gardeners cut deep holes in the concrete yard and then filled them with rich earth. The next day they planted a dozen mature cherry trees, one of which stood outside Jason's cell. He could see it from the tiny window. It wasn't long before some prisoners in Jason's block began to take bets on whether the tree would bloom or not.

To herald spring, a shower of downy, pink blossoms appeared. Each day he watched butterflies and birds hover around the tree. Some of the birds became familiar and he gave them names. He thought of the tree as a prisoner too, trapped in the concrete of the yard. At least, he thought, when it grew larger its blossoms would be seen and enjoyed beyond the prison walls. It gave him an interest and helped him to forget his troubles. As the weeks passed, his involvement with the tree increased. He was aware of the tree's every phase and its changes with the seasons. It was as lovely to him dressed in its fluffy spring blossoms as it was in winter, when it was a bare skeleton. When the tree bore its first cherries he waited eagerly for them to ripen and delighted in the sweet fruit.

When his release neared, the other men spun a web of fantasy about their future freedom, but he was apprehensive about returning to the outside world. On the day of his release he went to the cherry tree, stood under it for a moment, patted its trunk and picked a large sprig of pink blossoms. Then he walked through the rusty iron gates of the prison without looking back.

At first, the world outside the prison looked new and strange to his eyes, but he soon adapted, and noticed colours, shapes and smells that he'd forgotten. His uncle offered him a room at the back of the large family house. Though his low mood persisted he worked as a builder's labourer. Three years after his release, his uncle died and left him sufficient money to buy a small plot of land in the outer suburbs. A few years later he had saved sufficient to build a house with the aid of a few friends from work. As soon as the foundations were laid, he bought a cherry tree just like the one in the prison yard. It was expensive but he couldn't imagine his life without it. With it planted close to the house, he would see it from his bedroom window. Once he moved in, the tree reawakened the feelings of security and protection it had given him in prison.

His low mood returned and he stayed in the house unable to face the outside world. There were times when he often expressed his unhappy thoughts aloud to the tree as he had when in jail. He was aware that his behaviour was odd and that he had become obsessed with the tree, but he was too miserable to care.

One crisp spring day when the cherry tree was in full bloom, he received an invitation from his oldest friend, Brian, to visit his farm. The two had known each other since school days and their ties were strong. He battled with his impulse to stay at home where he was safe but the invitation was tempting and he decided to accept it. He set out before sunrise. At first he drove hesitantly, unused to being away from home. Then he relaxed, enjoying the soft pink landscape in the early light. With fresh eyes, he viewed the grasses and trees stirring in the breeze and breathed the sweet morning air. The two old friends ate, drank and shared memories for many hours and without realising it, Jason resumed his former friendly, easy-going manner. It was the start of his move from his self-imposed jail.

Months later, after gaining a little more confidence, he left the house and talked to his neighbours and explored parts of the area he had not seen before. He bought a dog and took him for long walks. By then his attitude towards the cherry tree had changed. He still thought of it as an exquisite ornament in the garden but his attachment to it had lessened.

FOURTEEN

DEVELOPING SELF-ESTEEM, BEING AWARE OF PERFECTIONISM, THE NEED TO SEEK APPROVAL AND SELF-BLAME

Depression and dented self-esteem go hand in hand, intensifying your despair and causing you to see yourself as a failure in every important aspect of your life. Research has shown how low self-esteem influences depression, and some studies have suggested that depression works negatively to decrease self-esteem.

You may have felt unworthy, unwanted and of little value for so long that you've accept it as the truth. You are likely to be self-critical and doubt yourself, avoid challenges and focus on your limitations instead of your strengths. In company you may be apologetic and unassertive. Your relationships may be plagued by fear of criticism or rejection. If you are a perfectionist you may drive yourself to perform.

Case study

Robyn liked to draw and by the time she was six or seven she was drawing cats, dogs and horses. One day she drew a picture of a horse as a gift for her mother. She ran into the kitchen, full of enthusiasm and handed the picture to her mother.

"Don't bother me now," her mother answered shortly. "I'm cooking and my hands are full. I'll look at it later."

Robyn left the kitchen downcast. When her father came in from work, he found her drawing on the carpet. He bent down to kiss her and looked at the scattered papers. "My little girl has been busy," he said with a smile. Robyn pointed at the horse she had drawn for her mother. "Look Daddy. Look at the horse I did for Mummy."

"It's lovely, darling but the legs are too fat for a horse...give me the pencil and I'll fix it."

Reluctantly Robyn handed her father the coloured pencil. She sighed and wondered if he would ever be satisfied. She wasn't going to draw a horse again.

What causes low self-esteem?

Not feeling recognised as worthwhile

The view of yourself as worthless and unlovable may have originated from your childhood or formative years at school. Perhaps you were made to feel a failure and received little, if any, love or praise from your parents. Feelings of hurt and rejection may have caused you to try harder to win assurance and acceptance, but nothing you did seemed good enough. Though founded in the past, these emotions may form the mirror in which you now see yourself.

The need to be like others

We need to belong and be accepted. You may follow fashion, read the same books as your friends and serve accepted foods to your guests. Feeling different and isolated from the group may increase your feelings of unworthiness.

Basing your self-esteem on achievement

If you base your self-esteem on your achievements you are likely to find yourself under constant pressure to perform, for example, you may play a game of golf well and are temporarily satisfied. Others congratulate you but there is always the fear that your game could drop away next time. You may become anxious. If you fail to increase your score or come up with at least the same score next time you may feel that you are slipping and as a result your self-esteem may drop. But is a golf score an indication of who you are?

If you push yourself to achieve more to feel good about yourself, whether it is in your work or sport, your will feel under constant pressure, look ahead to the next test rather than enjoy each day. Goal setting during one's life is an important aspect of living but aiming for the goal and not getting pleasure along the way may make you disgruntled and disappointed with what you have.

The harder you work at turning around your unproductive thoughts, the quicker your self-perceptions will change. You can train yourself to change the feelings that damage your self-esteem by being aware of self-critical thoughts. Answer the thoughts. Talk back at them until you have a more reasonable way of assessing yourself and your performance.

Nurturing your self-esteem

- Stop trying to prove yourself.

- Realise that you don't have to be perfect to be worthwhile. You are a human being with your own frailties and strengths like others and just as worthy.

- Respect and care for yourself. You don't require permission from others to take care of yourself. Don't wait to be told that you deserve a rest or a holiday, learn to assess that yourself. Seek to identify what would fulfil and satisfy you on a deeper level, and think of some ways of achieving this. Above all, respect your own needs as you would the needs of others, and your self-esteem will grow.

PERFECTIONISM AND LOW SELF-ESTEEM

It's natural to want to do something to the best of your ability. It can motivate you to do things you wouldn't have thought were possible and enable you to persevere in tough circumstances. If you do well, you feel good and take pleasure in meeting high standards. Others remark on your skill and ability and it elevates your self-esteem. However when you feel that your best may not be good enough and you must do things perfectly or fail, you may be edging towards stress, anxiety or even depression. Perfectionism often runs in families where approval and love is given as a reward for achievement. It is fostered and occurs in corporate organisations and schools that are achievement oriented.

PERFECTIONISM	HEALTHY STRIVING FOR EXCELLENCE
Setting standards that are so high that they may be beyond your reach.	Setting high standards within reach.
Only perfection will satisfy you.	You can accept the occasional error. The process is more important to you than the final product.
Being upset and defensive if criticised.	Seeing constructive criticism as an opportunity for self-improvement.
Fearing future failure.	More concerned with current activity.
Easily disheartened if things go wrong and unable to continue.	Able to bounce back and start again.
Seeing mistakes, inability to produce within a time frame as signs of failure and unworthiness.	Able to take small failures or errors in your stride.

Are you a perfectionist?

Perfectionism becomes more than a useful character trait and turns destructive when:

- You worry about your mistakes and don't give yourself credit for your successes. You have to reach that high level of perfection or you cannot consider yourself successful.

- You regret things you've done in the past that have not turned out as you would've liked. The thought of past failure is unbearable.

- You frequently criticise and find fault in others. If others can't meet your high standards you would rather do things yourself.

- If you fail you would rather give up and let your goal go.

- You don't even attempt things you fear you can't do perfectly. You believe that the shame of failing would be awful.

- Being perfect and number one is what's important. If you fail you'd rather forget your goal.

- You double check your work for errors, review your work repeatedly, and make small changes and put more work in than the task requires.

Overcoming perfectionism

Perfectionism is a difficult aspect of personality to overcome. It will take conscious effort to focus on your unproductive thinking and make positive changes. These are some suggestions:

- Accept that as a human being you need to forgive yourself for your mistakes, weaknesses and failings.

- Realise others also have weaknesses, limitations and failings and also make errors.

- Think of your mistakes as an opportunity to learn. Reward yourself for slight progress.

- Realise when your expectations are unrealistic. You might find that adjusting your standards slightly will make you a happier person.

- Realise when others' expectations of you are unrealistic, and they may be taking advantage of you.

- Become more aware that your excessive work and checking is of no particular value and merely increases your work level. It may even become stressful.

- Live in the present moment, enjoying your efforts instead of only aiming for an end result.

- Above all try to be more flexible and able to change your approach and plans.

THE NEED TO SEEK APPROVAL

If you assess your need to seek approval rationally, you will realise that it's the way *you* perceive yourself that really counts. Disapproval from others may be due to their own biases and have nothing to do with you. The following table demonstrates how you can question yourself rationally about your approval seeking.

APPROVAL SEEKING

QUESTION	RATIONAL ANSWER
How can I be sure that my friends accept and approve of me?	I'll never really know if they accept and approve of me or not. But they have befriended me so they must like something about me.
Does it make me inadequate and useless if they don't approve of me?	If they don't accept and approve of me it doesn't make me a failure. Although it would be nice if they did, I don't need their acceptance and approval to feel good about myself.
Will they be upset if I don't help out at the party?	They probably won't notice if I help out or not. Even if they do notice, it won't change the way they feel about me.
What will they think of me if I leave the party with Arthur?	They will probably be pleased for me, but it doesn't really matter.
Will they approve of Arthur?	It doesn't matter if they do or don't approve of him as long as I do. My opinion is the one that matters.

SELF–BLAME, SHAME AND GUILT

Many depressed people's thoughts are steeped in paralysing guilt and shame about minor transgressions.

These feelings can be so powerful that you believe that others could find out how flawed you are and reject you. Shame and guilt can make you feel isolated, different from other people and an outsider. Whether these thoughts are about your appearance, sexual desires or something that happened in the past, they can accentuate feelings of self-loathing.

Experiences from the past that shame deeply such as abuse are not easy to put aside and often cause lifelong feelings of guilt.

Realise that your feelings of guilt and shame are generated to a large extent by your depression and negative thoughts. Try a rational approach, even though it may seem difficult. In the following table you will find an example of guilt and shame being refuted with rational thinking. Acceptance and time will help you to look at yourself more clearly.

REVERSE THOUGHTS AND FEELINGS
OF GUILT, SHAME AND BLAME

GUILTY, SHAMING, BLAMING THOUGHT	RATIONAL RESPONSE
My house is untidy and friends came by. I'm ashamed of the mess. They'll think I'm a bad housewife.	My friends came to see me and not my house. If they can't accept some mess they are not really friends. Having a mess in my house doesn't mean that I'm a useless housewife.
I feel guilty about my sexual fantasies.	Everyone has sexual fantasies. I am going to try to enjoy them.
It's my fault that I lost my job. I should've tried even harder.	The company was downsizing and had to let most of the staff go. My loss of a job had nothing at all to do with my ability.

Separate your past from your present.

- Review the patterns that formed your need for approval and try to prevent yourself from re-creating past scenes. Your insight can help you to understand that you are different now and that others can't hurt you in the way they once did. Slowly you will learn to live in the light of the present rather than in the darkness of the past.

- To gain approval, you may try too hard to please others and deny your own needs. Decide whether your actions are motivated by choice.

- Listen in to the "shoulds" telling you how to live your life and what to believe and feel and let go of them. They are the demands of others that you have absorbed. Replace them with what seems right for you.

What if you are at fault?

After assessing a situation where you objectively find yourself to blame, rather than feeling guilty, consider taking positive action. Perhaps an apology is called for or some form of making amends.

Healing story: *The Winding River*

She scanned the wide expanse of water and sighed. Her eyes brimmed with tears of relief. At last she was aboard the sampan and her search for a new life had begun. Shivering in the icy wind, she pulled her woollen cap well down over her long, black hair and curled up under the narrow cover. She felt warmer and as the boat rocked she began to drift back to the events that had led to her journey.

***

Su Chi and her father, Su Mai ate their simple fish meal together each night.On the first Saturday of each month, they sailed the sampan to the nearest town for their few supplies. Over the years, Su Mai had taught his daughter to sail the sampan in all weathers, to fish and to prepare and cook the catch. During the journey he encouraged her hopes and dreams for the future. "My daughter you are quick and clever for your age and one day you'll move away from this village and make a good life."

She would smile and nod but she found difficulty in accepting the glowing image her father had of her or his hopes for her future. One morning, Su Mai was out walking along the river's edge, when he slipped on the mud and broke his hip. He was recovering well in hospital when pneumonia struck. Within a week he died.

Su Chi mourned for a month and then according to her father's wishes scattered his ashes over his favourite spot on the river. She believed that when his spirit found peace he would descend, to rest eternally on the riverbed. Each day, she walked along the riverbank grieving, her tears mingling with the water. The metal box where he had kept his money was almost empty. Sadly she realised that the sampan was all he had left her of any worth. At fifteen, with no experience to fit her for work, very soon she would be unable to pay the rent for the small house or afford food.

Though her father had told her that her uncle was a mean-spirited man, she had no alternative but to accept his offer of food and shelter. As she had feared, her uncle showed her no respect and treated her like a servant. After completing her chores for the day, she walked along the river. She felt her father near and had encountered his spirit several times.

His last message to her was clear: "Leave my brother's home; take the sampan and journey along the river to the city."

At first she ignored the message though she had lived near the river for many years and was accustomed to its faces and moods and was unafraid of sailing. She had lost her former zest and a journey along the water seemed pointless. It was when her uncle waved a stick in the air threatening to beat her if she didn't work faster, that she decided to take her father's advice. One pearly morning, she loaded the sampan with provisions stolen from her uncle's pantry. With her load, she waded into the cold water and then pushed the craft into the river.

For many days there was enough of a breeze for the sampan to sail. At night her thoughts were of her father, and her hope was that she would not disappoint him. She had completed more than half of the journey, when the sky darkened, wind swirled and currents raged. The suddenness and ferocity of the storm terrified her and she feared that the small craft constructed from only from a few planks, would be torn apart. She made certain of the wind's direction and used the long sculling oar to steer the boat to the river bank. Exhausted, she wound her coat closer and waited for the storm to pass. Would she manage to reach the city she wondered, as she stared up at the starless sky.

By morning the sky was clear and the waters still once more. She heaved the sampan back into the water. After several days of calm sailing, loud thumping woke her. When she rummaged through her father's simple tools, she found a torch, extra batteries, nails, a hammer and twine. The noise led her to a loose plank. Fortunately her father had taught her how to mend the sampan and in the torchlight she joined the planks with twine and used nails and the hammer to secure them.

Crafts of all sizes sailed the river, the route between outlying villages and the city. Boat owners passed each other with friendly greetings and waves. They were willing to help a stranded sailor or mend a boat.

Late one afternoon while admiring the light glinting on the river as it wound into the valley below, she noticed a nearby fishing boat rocking fiercely. She lowered the sail and edged towards it. A man called out for help. Apparently minutes earlier, his brother had tried to reel in a large fish, but had lost his footing, become entangled in his line and was drawn into the depths. The distraught man on deck could not rescue his brother alone and had almost given up hope of freeing him.

Su Chi kicked off her boots, and dived into the water. At first all she could see were fish and sea grasses. She was about to surface when she noticed a large scaly creature writhing as it struggled to free itself from a hook and line. It wasn't a fish, but a dragon of sorts similar to ones in her early storybooks. The man ensnared by his line, hung limply. She knew she had to act fast. Years of fishing had made her adept with a rope and knife. She circled the creature, distracting it by flicking her shiny knife in front of its eyes. When it ceased its thrashing, she immobilised it with the rope. The fisherman jumped into the water to free the man still caught on his line. Carefully they lifted him to the surface. While the fisherman attempted to revive him, she cut the creature free. On returning to the deck the fisherman was holding his dead brother in his arms and weeping.

The rest of Su Chi's journey continued without incident, apart from the shoals of fish that swam alongside the sampan as a guard of honour. When tall buildings beckoned in the distance, she knew that she had almost reached her destination. In the months that followed, she noticed a gradual change in herself. Though her courage was known to all on the river and some further afield, more important was her changed view of herself. She felt more at peace and open to new experiences and pleasures.

Now that his daughter no longer needed his guidance, the spirit of Su Chi's father sank to the riverbed where he rested forever. The dragon-like creature was never seen on the river again.

FIFTEEN
※

MOVING FROM ANGER TO ASSERTIVENESS

Anger and depression are closely connected. You feel more angry than usual when you are feeling down? And when you're angry you may fuel a down mood. Anger is a normal healthy emotion, a natural survival instinct that allows you to build up sufficient energy to retaliate when threatened or protect yourself if attacked. However, if anger gets out of control, you can find yourself at the mercy of a destructive, unpredictable force that can cause upheaval in every sphere of your life. Anger is a powerful emotion that you can feel building throughout your body. Often it is a motivating force that calls for action.

Case study

Angela, aged nineteen, was unemployed and depressed. She had suffered depression for three years and had trouble coping with part-time work during that period. The company she worked for was in financial difficulty and along with about ninety others she was made redundant. She was angry and resentful about her job loss.

"I don't know why they let me go. I tried so hard and put in as much effort and time as the others. It's typical of my life. I can't win. I'm never in the right place at the right time. If bad luck's going to happen, well here I am waiting for it. It makes me so angry." She couldn't let her anger go and thought about the loss of the job all the time. "I don't think it was fair of them to sack me. I doubt I'll ever get another job now. Anyway, why bother if the same thing will happen to me again." She felt hot all over and wiped her brow. "So they think they can just push people around. They'll be sorry one day."

A few weeks later when she had an interview for another job, she made nasty remarks about her ex employer and didn't get the job. No one likes a complaining angry person.

Inability to express anger

Many depressed people are filled with anger and resentment that they are unable to express. Fear of confrontation and concerns about losing control may lead to suppression of the anger. If the reason for anger remains unresolved, it may fester and cause long-term resentment. Unresolved anger may also lead to the unleashing of fury or blaming yourself and causing guilt feelings.

Depression may lower your tolerance to stress so that even a slight or relatively minor incident or situation can elicit disproportionate frustration and even anger, for example, a car not starting in the morning, a washing machine breaking down, slow traffic, an argument with a friend or co-worker, or dislike of company policy.

Anger and resentment in relationships

Resentment and hostility in relationships can often do a great deal of harm. Depression may make you feel especially vulnerable, so that you may strike out in defence about small irritations. You are likely to be withdrawn and uncommunicative and it is difficult for a partner to reach out to comfort you. In this mood, resentments and frustration can build to unrealistic proportions.

Insecurity may take the form of feared unfaithfulness or loss of love, and result in your need for continual reassurance. Rows concerning insecurity may be frequent and vicious. For example, questioning a partner about extra time spent at work or with friends.

Anxious about rejection and low in self-esteem, you may act irrationally– incensed, question the future of a relationship or even leave a partner. At the time leaving may seem easier to cope with than being discarded. Many people split up while they are stressed or depressed and review the situation differently when calm returns and they have more insight. It can take a supportive, insightful partner to make a relationship with a depressed person work.

Is being angry and irritable inherited or learned?

This is a matter of continuing debate among experts. It is known that within some families there are traceable close relatives who are easily angered. It is uncertain yet whether this leaning towards aggression and anger in families also exists in families that have a known hereditary line of depression

Anger and resentment related to the past

Much anger and resentment stems from the past, from childhood memories, grievances about unloving or uncaring parents or unfair treatment at school or at work. Unhealed wounds from the past can be so damaging that they intrude, constantly filling thoughts with memories of being unloved and unworthy or unequal to others. These chronic, insistent self-destructive thoughts can add to your depressed feelings and slow recovery. Resentful feelings are often expressed in fantasies and dreams.

Case study

In his counselling session, Danny spoke about his resentment and hostility towards his mother: "My mother's on my mind most nights as I struggle to fall asleep. I run over and over the time I was only three or four years old. I remember her pushing me away because she didn't want me around and yelling at me to *keep quiet...get lost* when she was busy. I can't recall a single time that she held me, caressed me or told me a bedtime story. I had to keep very quiet so as not to bother her and if I cried she'd hit me.

Danny swallowed hard before continuing. "She never made me feel loved or wanted and now I despise her for it. I fantasise about making her suffer for what she's done to me. Sometimes I imagine pulling out her long blonde hair one strand at a time. I had a daydream a few months ago...I killed her. It was scary that I felt so good afterwards. Of course I'd never have done something like that as much as I resented her. I'm not the violent sort."

He wiped away a few tears. "I know my resentment towards her is not helping me; it's not making me like myself more. Every single relationship I've had with a woman hasn't worked out. I'm twenty-eight and I still feel insecure. I've ruined relationships because I don't trust a woman to love me....and I'm jealous and possessive. Nobody likes that."

He stopped and stared at the carpet. "I've tried to understand that my mother had a hard life herself and didn't know how to love, but I still can't forgive her. It wasn't my fault."

Managing anger

So many things contribute to uncontrolled anger – feelings and thoughts at the time, the pressures experienced and unresolved past issues, all have bearing on a tendency to become enraged. Before attempting to manage your anger, you need to be honest with yourself and admit to feelings of hurt and fear.

Pinpointing your anger triggers

Depression can make experiences appear more negative and can cause you to anticipate the worst outcome in any situation. Being able to be aware of your triggers and prevent your anger at this early stage will make your thinking more rational and your mood calmer.

If you find it difficult to pinpoint your particular vulnerabilities, discuss this topic with a friend or relative who knows you well, or seek counselling. Look at the things that trigger an angry outburst at home, work and in social situations. Being aware of these will be of tremendous help to you. Remind yourself about these points from time to time, so that if you are in an angry state you will have these thoughts as a familiar source of reasoning.

Ask yourself these questions

- How important the issues that anger you now will be in a week or by tomorrow? Soon the argument and the reasons for your anger may blur and seem inconsequential. Is it worth being agitated and brooding over slights or hurts?

- Some issues that anger you may be central to your beliefs and values and of a crucial nature, such as a person who insults you in public or questions your morality. You may feel angry about being charged the wrong price for some goods or furious that a neighbour suggested you weren't telling the truth. Rage will not serve any purpose. You need to be coolly rational, direct and incisive in your response and develop a plan of action.

- What are you hoping to prove? Do you always have to be right? Do you need to win at all costs? If you don't win or you are wrong this time, does it mean that you are a lesser person? What does winning mean anyway? Is it worth the effort?

- If you are blaming yourself for someone else's hurt or anger, realise that you do not have to take on this responsibility. That person owns his own behaviour and feelings.

- Do things always have to be perfect? Life isn't always fair and things don't always pan out as you would like them to, but is your emotional reaction going to help you cope with changes or adaptations you need to make?

Practical methods of controlling anger

Some of the following practical methods are common sense – others are a little more complex. You can use a combination of these techniques or any of them on their own.

- *Slowing down.* Slow yourself down and don't jump to conclusions. Make sure you've listened carefully and assessed the situation. Take time to think through your response, before you regret what you've said. Rational thought is the most effective method of controlling anger in situations that upset and annoy you and it is also the best approach towards genuine concerns or grievances.

- *Counting* to 5 or 10, before you respond in a heated discussion is a well-tested method of keeping your anger in check.

- *Deep breathing.* Taking a few deep breaths to calm you down will allow you time to gather perspective. Later you may decide to spend some time on deep breathing to ease the hyped-up feeling a surge of adrenaline brings when you are angry.

- *Relaxation* will allow you to return to a quiet, calm frame of mind. If you practice relaxation on a regular basis it will keep you even tempered and prevent your anger from firing at unimportant issues.

- *Writing a journal.* You may be angry because of a serious illness in the family or a death that you find impossible to accept. This type of anger, fired by painful feelings of unfairness, injustice or even remorse, can be eased by writing down your feelings every day.

- *Activity.* Sometimes activity helps to dissipate long-term and buried anger. Going to the gym, working in the garden or shed often helps. Scream out loud a few times. When the feelings become intense, hitting your pillow is an old standby.

- *Creative pursuits.* Activities like pottery, painting, craftwork, writing, poetry, cabinet making or furniture restoration may ease long-term or buried hurts.

Moving away from anger to assertiveness

Expressing your anger in an assertive and acceptable manner has many advantages. Assertiveness is a direct means of expressing anger while you remain in control. Being assertive is not a form of weakness, passivity or "backing off", but rather a way of expressing your needs without hostility or infringing the rights of others. Assertiveness means that you won't lose your self-respect, act or say things you will be ashamed of later. It helps you to remain in control of your life and enables you to stand up for the things you value and believe in. It is likely to give you a better chance of proving your point

Leaning to be assertive

How can you give vent to your feelings in a way that you and others will find acceptable?

Like any other skill, assertiveness takes time to learn and a desire to move away from aggression. You will have to be patient with yourself.

There may be issues that prevent you from moving forward. These are some of the factors that could still be in your way:

- *Making a mistake:* Ask yourself: Does it matter if you make a mistake? Are your friends always correct? Focus on the things you do well and your unique qualities.

- *Approval:* You will have to accept that you cannot always have others' approval. We all have different views and values. You need to decide what is important for you.

- *Constructive criticism:* Consider who made the judgement and if it is constructive. Constructive feedback is always helpful. You will have to decide whether you wish to accept it or not.

- *Rejection:* None of us escape rejection. It is important to realise that not everyone can like you or that you will like every person you come across. If you are rejected from one person or group it doesn't follow that you will be rejected by others. Rather than to be angry and hurt review the situation and try to learn from it. Consider if there is anything you need to change about your own behaviour.

Fear of saying "no"

It is important to be able to disagree in some situations. Being able to say "no"when you are asked to do something you don't agree with can prove essential to your safety and your integrity.

Fear of reverting to aggression

If you are angry with someone, it can be hard to honestly express your feelings. Listen and show the respect you would like. Be objective and describe your reasons factually and avoid exaggeration or being judgmental. Always attempt to compromise and do not dominate the conversation. Being assertive may mean that your views may not be accepted or liked. At least you will feel that you have behaved in an acceptable manner and you will be able to walk away with self-respect.

Healings story: *The Blue Venetian Vase*

Nina peeled off her coat. A heat surge had created two pink patches on her cheeks. She sighed and soaked up beads of perspiration.

It was her lunch break and she wandered into the nearby shopping mall. A gift shop tucked into a corner caught her attention. A few pieces of pottery and some bric-a-brac were attractively arranged in the cramped window. She stepped inside to view the once-loved treasures more closely – an ornate silver brush and comb set, a tapestry footstool, fancy cups, plates and familiar ornaments that stirred her memory of days past and people now gone. A white fluted dish with a braided handle caught her eye and she smiled. Her great aunt Bettie once had one just like it and kept it filled with sweets and chocolates. A group of tiny figurines reminded her of her grandmother's prized collection of miniature ornaments kept behind glass, in a prominently placed dresser in the sitting room. As a child, a tiny pair of blue and gold shoes and a dancing lady that fitted into the palm of her hand, fascinated her.

When admiring a blue vase, she was overwhelmed by a heat surge. In her haste to pull up the sleeves of her jumper, she knocked over the vase. It lay shattered on the floor. Though she rarely cried, tears trickled down her cheeks. The unusual intensity of emotion and the changes she was undergoing had begun only a few weeks earlier. As the shop owner swept up the glass, Nina's tears subsided. She calmed herself, stood awkwardly for a while and then looked around the shop. She decided to buy an old ginger jar. Once she had paid for it and the broken vase, she rushed back to work.

When she unwrapped the jar that evening, she noticed a flaw in the pattern. One stem of leaves pointed upwards and not down like all the others. She moved it around the room until she was satisfied that the best place for it was on top of the wooden cabinet in front of a decorative mirror.

Curiosity made her lift the jar's lid. Inside was a dried posy of strawflowers and a few forget-me-nots, tied with a faded, red, satin ribbon. Carefully she lifted the posy. It was extremely old, but the faded petals had survived. She turned it about in her hand and wondered who had hidden it there. Perhaps a young woman had received it from an admirer?

She replaced the lid and while placing the jar on the cabinet, she glanced at her reflection in the mirror. Her expression was tense but her skin was still unwrinkled. But in time it would dry and the colour of her hair would fade like the flowers.

During the next few days she thought about another jar she had noticed at the shop that would make an attractive partner to the first one. At the end of that week, she finished work a little earlier and hurried to the shop. She found one she wanted and took it to the counter. The owner of the shop was busy with another customer and her young daughter was on the floor playing with a smiling clown figurine.

"That's a lovely clown," Nina said.

The girl nodded. "He's my favourite... and Mum saved him for me," she said.

"Oh! How did she do that?"

"I dropped him on the floor and he broke into lots of tiny pieces. I couldn't stop crying, so Mum stuck all the bits together until he was fixed."

"You must've been very happy about that."

'Yes...but when the lady who comes to clean the house was dusting, she knocked him off the shelf. I thought he was broken again and couldn't be fixed."

She stroked the figurine. "But Mum stuck him together again and said that he was extra tough and now he could never break."

"Maybe that's why he's got such a big smile," Nina said. And they both laughed.

When Nina made her purchase, she asked the owner of the shop about the flaw in the pattern of the jar she'd bought earlier. "Some painters specially made mistakes to prove that they weren't perfect."

Nina was a little disappointed to find that the pattern on the second jar was flawless and nothing had been hidden in it. But the pair standing together on the cabinet looked attractive.

Weeks later she had a dream about the antique shop. Objects from the shop were in a circle in the moonlight. The sweet dish was bursting with sweets and chocolates, the figures and both jars were there. The first one she had bought was filled with fresh strawflowers tied with a red, satin ribbon. The child's clown figurine danced and pulled funny faces. A streak of moonlight caught the blue Venetian vase that she had dropped. It was whole now.

She awoke from the dream feeling rested. It was her first peaceful night without drenching sweats. Perhaps the real change is beginning, she thought.

PART 4

MINDFULNESS-BASED COGNITIVE THERAPY (MBCT)

SIXTEEN

THE ESSENCE OF MINDFULNESS-BASED COGNITIVE THERAPY (MBCT)

Mindfulness-based cognitive therapy (MBCT) is a popular, highly regarded and successful method of self-awareness training that was developed by Williams, Teasdale, Segal and Kabat-Zinn and provides another valuable path in understanding the link between thinking and feeling. It is derived to a large part from ancient concepts found in many spiritual and religious beliefs, such as Buddhism, Hinduism, Judaism and Taoism. It combines these ancient concepts with skills found in cognitive behavioural therapy (CBT). The aim is healing depression and preventing relapses.

Comparing mindfulness-based cognitive therapy (MBCT) with cognitive behavioural therapy (CBT)

In essence, cognitive behavioural therapy (CBT) attempts to teach a person to identify their destructive or irrational thoughts, to understand how the thoughts make them feel, and to replace them with more constructive and reality-based thinking.

Mindfulness-based cognitive therapy (MBCT) focuses on awareness of incoming thoughts and physical sensation *in the moment*, accepting them but not responding or reacting to them. Thus past and present events or experiences are acknowledged but not judged, analysed or challenged.

You may remember the section on CBT that explains how depressed thinking is linked to negative automatic thinking. Automatic thoughts and images are those thoughts that seem to pop up into consciousness or are habitual ways of thinking based on the past. They influence the way you interpret your world. Automatic thoughts have their dangers because they are rarely questioned and accepted as true. When CBT is used as a therapy, these negative thoughts are challenged or changed into more reality based or constructive thoughts.

Now, when using MBCT, you let go of those unproductive thoughts instead of challenging them, judging them or trying to push them out of conscious awareness. You focus your attention on the present moment. For example, imagine your thoughts are being beamed from an annoyingly loud and critical television programme. Using mindfulness you don't have to change channels, turn the television off or leave the room, you alter the way you listen and watch the sounds and images so that they no longer bother you.

One of the reasons that mindfulness techniques have become so widespread, is that once the basics are mastered, the therapy can be adapted to be used anywhere and at any time, while walking or at work, or even while doing the dishes and cleaning the house. It is about appreciating and accepting being alive. It can be used safely with any medication a doctor prescribes and other therapies if desired. It will not conflict with any religious beliefs, culture or regimen.

Case study

Jenny was washing up the dishes after dinner. While her hands encased in rubber gloves scrubbed away at the dirt, her mind was elsewhere, switching from one topic to another. She began thinking of all the things she had failed to accomplish that day. Then she was thinking of the glass beads she had to sew on to a costume for her daughter Meredith's dancing. She realised how tired she was but pushed the heavy feeling away. She realised she hadn't put the washing machine on as she needed all the cotton clothing in the heat. She left her gloves on, darted to the laundry and returned to finish off in the kitchen.

When Tony, her husband called out to ask her if she was finished in the kitchen, the jolt of his loud voice startled her and she dropped a cup. It fell to the floor and broke into pieces. She muttered to herself as she swept up the porcelain shards. She was returning the vacuum to the cupboard when the broken cup reminded her of breaking her mother's favourite teapot when she was about eight. She had been given a hiding for that and she remembered how it hurt. The greater hurt was that her mother was angry with her for days and went on and on about losing her favourite teapot. Jenny remembered how sad she felt when she thought about the teapot being more important to her mother than she was.

When her daughter asked Jenny a question, she didn't hear it. She was lost in the past. Her daughter walked off in a huff and Jenny didn't notice that either. Clearly Jenny had too many thoughts crowding her mind and was not in the present and not concentrating or she wouldn't have broken the cup or ignored her daughter.

Overcome with exhaustion and the sadness that had been with her for months, she went to bed. But she couldn't sleep, guilt about not fixing her daughter's costume nagged at her, but too tired to get up, she lay there. "What's wrong with me she said to herself between her tears? I'm such a mess...can't get anything right lately."

The key principles of mindfulness-based cognitive therapy:

1. Purposeful awareness

2. Acceptance

3. Flexibility and openness

4. Compassion

5. Meditation – letting go

1. Purposeful awareness

If you are purposely aware, you are intentionally paying attention to what you are thinking and experiencing now, in the moment.

For example, while you are drinking a cup of coffee, you might also have the television on, someone is talking to you and you pick up a magazine to glance at the cover. You know you are drinking the coffee, the cup is in your hand but there are many distractions. You are involving yourself in too many things at the same time for you to be purposely aware of the process of drinking the coffee. You miss the sensation of swirling the hot liquid in your mouth, the rich taste of the coffee, the feel of the porcelain cup against your mouth, the pleasure of the experience. Knowing you are drinking the coffee is different from drinking it mindfully.

Do you recognise yourself in any of these examples of distraction?

- You may become so distracted that you are no longer present or participating? People around you may notice and feel ignored or upset.

- Part of a conversation seems to drift away and you lose the thread.

- You go to a room to do something but forget why you are there.

- You are so distracted while driving that you forget whether you have taken the correct route or not.

- You can't remember where you have put things.

- You forget that a pot is cooking and it boils over.

- You put your glasses or car keys in the fridge or other places.

In a depressed frame of mind, it is common to ruminate, think in a circular way. You might begin by thinking about why you feel down and hope to arrive at a solution. But instead of coming up with an answer you may begin to rehash the problem, turn it this way and that. Your thoughts become negative as you link issues to past events and possible future fears. An even more unproductive cycle of thinking often results.

Mindfulness brings you back to experiencing the present moment, not to the past or the future. So you are directing your attention to what is happening *now*. Of course you can and should think about the past or future but when you choose to do so specifically...mindfully. In the present moment you can enjoy life more intensely and appreciate things you may have overlooked before.

2. **Acceptance**

Most unpleasant thoughts and emotions occur automatically as learned responses to comments or actions by parents or other significant others that may go back to childhood. Instead of battling to control them, you can accept these difficult and unpleasant thoughts and use your energy for the things you can control. You don't have to try to escape from them, push them aside or try to distract yourself. You don't need to judge them as good or bad or become distressed. You can let them be but not respond to them. Whether thoughts are pleasant or unpleasant you observe them mindfully and step back from your emotions.

3. **Flexibility and openness**

Conscious awareness allows you to be more flexible, to experience more widely and deeply. You can notice your thoughts without reacting to them, be more open and consider experimenting with new ideas or revisit old ones in novel ways. When you are in the moment, you are more responsive to free floating ideas and creative solutions emerge and evolve. Destructive thoughts need no longer be taken as the truth about yourself. Being more flexible means you can now move on.

4. **Compassion**

Compassion is often described as understanding another's thoughts and feelings or standing in someone else's shoes. Mindfulness takes this definition further by encouraging you to develop compassion for yourself, connect with yourself, listen to your own feelings and experiences and gain self-knowledge. It allows you to stop judging yourself or struggling to achieve perfection and learn to trust your feelings. Using mindfulness can help you become more aware and gentle in response to any guilt or trauma reactions.

5.   Meditation – letting go

The form of letting go in mindfulness training usually involves regular meditation. Mindfulness meditation will teach you how to stay in the present and utilise the meditation technique in your daily activities. It will also help you to increase your awareness of how your thoughts affect your body and emotions. Meditation is useful in assisting you with emotional and health issues by encouraging a calm relaxed approach and preventing a build-up of anxiety.

Healing story: *Looking for trouble*

Lynne was on holiday with friends, elated and enjoying herself. Only three weeks earlier she had been so depressed that she could barely drag herself out of bed. Mood swings had caused havoc in her life and had even brought her close to suicide.

This is Lynne's story:
"I was having a great time until the second week of my holiday. A few of us went to a disco we hadn't been to before. We heard it was good fun. I took extra care with my appearance and dressed in my favourite outfit, a red low-cut dress with high-heeled shoes. I was flying high, having a ball on the dance floor when I met Kevin – blond, green-eyed and muscular. We danced all evening and during the break he dipped his hand into his bag and offered me an ecstasy tablet. I refused, and it was just as well. I would have been really ill, in that high mood. We danced until the early hours and decided to spend the night together.

When we left the disco I saw cops hanging around but I didn't make anything of it. About five minutes later a police van swooped up. When they opened Kevin's bag it was full of tablets. Then they looked in my handbag and I was stunned. It was packed with marijuana. Kevin must have put the stuff in there while I was in the toilet. Of course I was shocked and upset but I couldn't do a thing. Not then anyway. They took us both to the station for questioning and we were charged with drug dealing.

They held me in their lockup till morning. It was a small cold cell with a hard bed but I was so tired that I could have slept anywhere. I'd been too hyped to sleep more than three hours a night for a week or so and the tiredness caught up with me. I woke later and lay there thinking about how Kevin had used me, and was furious with myself for being taken in by him. Before nodding off, I noticed a row of letters carved into the cell wall spelling the name JANIE. I touched them and a mist appeared. It took a while for a form to be clear enough...and then there before me stood a plump, elderly woman, dressed in an old-fashioned prison uniform.

Thanks for calling me up, dearie, I'm a bad old girl, but I've come to see you tonight, to help you. Let me see, I think I was in this lock-up at least five times. I can tell you, it was so miserable in here that I realised that if I didn't take control of my life, others would. Most of the time, I was just like you, always unsure, never knowing what the next day would bring. My moods were like the weather, always changing.

I rubbed my eyes and shook my head hard but the image hadn't shifted. *My family used to fill me up with horrid-tasting herbal potions to calm me down when I was extra happy, and then let me weep for hours until my sad phases passed. That's something I don't want to remember, if you know what I mean, dearie. Goodness gracious, when I think of it, the endless pressure made me feel as if the devil himself was in my head. At least where I am now, I have peace.*

The woman's high-pitched voice rattled on. *Dearie, I wouldn't like to tell you all the things I did without a thought when I was in a high-rolling mood. I couldn't stop talking, and then there was my spending and gambling. It should never have happened, and I was wise afterwards. I didn't have much control. Anyway, one day when I was riding the crest of a wave, I stole a beautiful dress from a fancy shop. Why, you may ask. Well, I was so happy and I wanted it. I stole a few more things later and they were pretty too. That's how I ended up here. I suppose I had to learn the hard way. I shudder when I think of the way the cops treated me when they caught me. Ugh! I notice some of them haven't improved that much these days. I kicked up a fuss when they locked me up. When they couldn't handle me they sent me to a place where crazy women howled, strapped me in a straitjacket and threw me into a tiny, tight cell.*

I shuddered and wished the apparition would leave but she went on talking. *Before I go, dearie, I must share with you what I learned about this problem...of ours. First of all, when your mood spirals up, stay in a quiet place. You don't want too much excitement or noise to stir you even more. It's a marvellous time to write down your good ideas or you won't catch them again with so much going on in your head. When you swing down and you feel sad, be kind to yourself. After all, if you don't look after yourself, who will?*

Waggling a fat finger at me, she emphasised her point. *You know, I recall so well the sweet and calming smell of lavender. Nothing like my grandmother's recipes for relaxing. Of course, there are those really dreadful times when none of that helps and what you really need is a good doctor. So, there you have it from an old mood swinger, my love.*

The small, plump woman stood on her toes, raised her rounded body, twirled about twice and then disappeared. I drifted into sleep and dreamt about her, Kevin and the drugs. The din in the cells woke me and Janie was on my mind again. Was she a ghost or just part of my imagination? Whoever or whatever she was, she'd come to help me when I was afraid. I hadn't taken my mood swings seriously, but she made me realise that I could do something about them.

Kevin did the right thing in the end and admitted that he had put the marijuana in my handbag and they let me go. On the bus back to the motel I could feel a cool wind blowing inside me. I was heading for a downer and it was time for me to go home."

SEVENTEEN
❈

MINDFULNESS DEEP BREATHING AND MEDITATION

Breath control is an intrinsic part of many ancient oriental religions. For over 2,000 years the Chinese have practised the healing breathing regimens of Qi Gong, the Yogis call the healing breath pranayama, in Japan the Shintos call it *sakia-tundra*. The early Hindu scriptures, the *Upanishads,* written between 200 and 500 BC, assert that: *The breath of life is greater than hope. For just as the spokes [of a wheel] are fixed in the hub, so is everything fixed in this breath of life.*

Deep breathing is a good place to start learning about mindfulness. Even a few minutes of deep breathing during the day will make a difference to the way you feel.

"Take a deep breath and relax," is a popular remedy for stress. Although it may seem too simple an answer, it works. Deep breathing has a profound calming effect on distressed emotions and can ease the anxiety frequently associated with depression. When you're relaxed, you breathe slowly and rhythmically, but when you're tense your breathing is fast and shallow. Relaxation plays an important part in creating a sense of wellbeing and comfort. It decreases anxiety, allows sleep to occur more deeply and prevents a rapid build-up of stress. It also lessens muscle tension, lowers blood pressure and heart rate. Studies on the relaxation response indicate that metabolic rate is decreased and that the calming alpha wave increases activity in the brain. By controlling the pace and rhythm of your breathing, it is possible to change the way you feel.

Please Note: If you are in the midst of a deep or severe depression please do not attempt these mindfulness exercises on your own or consider downloading CDs for mindfulness relaxation. This might worsen and not assist your condition. This form of meditation for severely depressed people is best performed within a group situation run by an experienced mindfulness practitioner, or individually with a psychologist trained in this method of therapy. Meditation can at times unleash hurtful thoughts or remind you of experiences that are difficult to deal with alone. Therefore I recommend that if you suffer from severe depression it would be best to consult your doctor, psychologist or psychiatrist before embarking on mindfulness-based cognitive therapy on your own.

MINDFULNESS DEEP BREATHING

Though you breathe in and out all day and night you are usually not aware of the experience of breathing. One of the ways of learning more about mindful awareness is to become conscious of your breathing. You will discover how awareness of your breathing will deepen from daily practice. Even a few minutes of deep breathing during the day will make a huge difference.

In this exercise you breathe "in" and "out" as usual, but do not change your rhythm or make any particular effort. You simply concentrate on your breathing and nothing else – on the movement in your body, the feeling in your lungs, the warmth of the breath on your face as you exhale.

At first you will find concentrating on your breathing for this brief time surprisingly difficult. Your mind might drift to all sorts of topics and refuse to concentrate on your breathing. Do not be disappointed. Instead, try to practice during that day and on following days. Gradually you will find yourself able to concentrate on your breath and be aware of the sensation. Your thoughts will no longer jump about and you will not notice sounds around you.

Hyperventilation or over breathing

It is important to be aware of hyperventilation, the unpleasant physical reaction that results from receiving too much oxygen from over breathing. A loss of carbon dioxide from the blood occurs and this can lead to increased heart rate and rapid breathing. Other symptoms of hyperventilation include feeling unable to catch your breath, confusion, dizziness, headache, light headedness, trembling, tingling in fingers and toes and hot and cold flushes.

If you are tense and anxious to start with, experiencing these strange and uncomfortable physical symptoms will only intensify anxiety. It makes good sense to begin to breathe more slowly and in a relaxed way.

Patience

Be patient with yourself as you learn to master the techniques of deep breathing. After a few weeks of practice it will feel natural and become part of your daily life. It can lower high stress levels and help you to cope with the anxiety that often occurs together with a depressed mood.

This breathing exercise is the first important exercise in mindfulness and will start you on your path to further and deeper forms of mindfulness training.

MINDFULNESS MEDITATION

Staying in the present

Mindfulness training involves disciplining your mind to stay in the present moment. Meditation in the present prevents you from drifting back to the past or moving to the future. It also controls the obsessive rumination common in depression and anxiety and encourages calm. With meditation you become increasingly aware, sensing sounds, smells and sights around you. You learn to experience directly, notice warmth or coolness, how your body reacts when you move instead of thinking about it. Once you have learned to stay in the present, you can use the technique in your daily activities. It will help you to increase your awareness of your thoughts and how they in turn affect your body and emotions. Through becoming more mindful of your thoughts and how you respond to them you will be able to be more rational and make choices with greater clarity.

The concept of working mindfully

Some people find the concept of mindfulness difficult at first. To help you work with the concept, be aware of your thoughts, feelings, sensations, and how your body feels. The following table simplifies an experience of being aware of unpleasant thoughts and feeling.

AWARENESS OF THOUGHTS, FEELING AND SENSATIONS

Your experience or situation	Your thoughts	Your feelings	How your body feels	How you feel and think now
Sitting in a chair in the sun.	In the past… thinking of my mother crying.	Churned up, stressed Feel like crying	Tense	Still thinking about it. I'm very distressed.
Sitting in the same chair the following day	How I mucked up at work	Angry Sad	Heavy Sweaty	I am upset with myself and worried what will happen at work.

Starting to meditate mindfully

Exercise: 2–30 seconds: Sit comfortably and ask yourself what you are experiencing now. What are your thoughts, feeling and physical sensations?

Exercise: 1 minute: Sit comfortably and question yourself about your experiences at the moment. What are your thoughts, feeling and physical sensations? This time make all these observations without trying to change your thoughts or find answers.

Thought labelling

While you are meditating, during the day or when you are practising mindful awareness, you might catch yourself having non-productive thoughts or worrying. Though constructive problem solving is an important function for us all, constant circular worrying creates anxiety and produces no practical outcomes. Labelling your worries is a simple and relaxed method to cope with them.

Step 1
If you notice yourself worrying, instead of trying to change the thought or getting angry with yourself, simply label the thought as *just worrying*. It is important to use that exact term and not change it. It doesn't matter how many times you have found yourself worrying. Each time you catch yourself worrying you must use the same phrase *just worrying*. This is a non-judgemental statement, implying no criticism.

Step 2
Continue what you were doing applying the *just worrying* method when necessary.

Step 3
Once you are used to labelling your worries as *just worrying*, you can move on to giving a variety of names to specific types of worry as you notice them. The following table will provide some examples.

HOW TO LABEL WORRYING THOUGHTS

Thought	Type of thought	A helpful label
I should be more careful. Now I've made more mistakes.	Self-critical.	Just worrying about being self-critical.
If I would've started earlier, and studied the reference on page 23 in my book, I would've had far less trouble.	Analysing.	Just worrying about analysing.
That person doesn't like me. I can see it on his face.	Judging.	Just worrying about judging.

It doesn't matter how many times you catch yourself worrying in an hour or day. What is important is that realise that you are doing this. To help you to become more aware of worrying, try the labelling technique. It can be used for any disturbing or repetitive thought.

The following table illustrates how labels can be integrated into your thinking and feeling experience.

MINDFUL AWARENESS, AND LABELLING YOUR THOUGHTS

Your experience or situation	Labelling your thoughts	Your feelings	How your body feels now	How you feel and think now
Sitting in a chair in the sun.	The continual memory of my mother crying is me...*just worrying.*	I am no longer upset about mom crying. I've let it float away. I now feel very warm and comfortable. The chair feels so comfortable and I like relaxing.	Comfortable My breathing is slow and easy.	I am no longer upset.
Walking.	My persistent work thought is *just worrying.*	If I messed up, it happened and now I can let it pass. No good worrying. I am pleased that I went out for a walk. The air is very fresh. I needed the exercise.	Hot and sweaty.	I have let the worry about work go. I made a mistake. Will fix it at work tomorrow.

Moving on to deeper meditation

Once you have mastered the simple exercises in meditation move on to the "body scan meditation", the form of meditation recommended by the theorists and practitioners of mindfulness meditation.

Body scan mindfulness

1. Lie comfortably and close your eyes.

2. Once you have settled take a few moments to notice the way in which your body contacts the floor or bed.

3. Notice your breathing – the rhythm and pace of each in and out breath.

4. Do not try to change the pace of your breathing or place any expectations on yourself.

5. As you breathe in be aware of the air entering your nostrils, passing through your lungs and entering the abdomen. Concentrate on the left side of your body, and imagine the breath travelling all the way down your left leg and into your left foot and into the toes of that foot. Notice the sensations in your toes and then allow your breath to travel all the way back up your leg, through your abdomen and lungs and finally out through your nose. Try to continue doing this a few times, if you can. You might find this difficult or even strange or feel nothing but don't be concerned about it.

6. Now no longer focus on your toes. Take a deeper breath and turn your attention to the sole, instep, and heel of your left foot, noticing the sensations where your foot touches the bed or floor. Continue to breathe into and out of each part of your foot as you move on to explore your left ankle, the many bones of the foot. As you experience sensations in the different parts of your foot continue breathing into it and out.

7. Take a deep breath and let go of your foot completely as you begin to bring awareness into your lower left leg, your calf , shin knee, thigh and so on.

8. If your mind wanders, remind yourself to return to awareness of your breath and the area you were concentrating on.

9. Continue to maintain awareness of your breath as you move up your left leg and on to the rest of your body, noticing the feeling of that

particular part. As you move on to each area breathe into it on an "in" breath and out of it on an "out" breath.

10. Once you have "scanned" or visited each part of your body spend a few moments being aware of your total body, noticing your breathing as it flows through you.

After you have become accustomed to this method of meditation you might find that you are able to label your worries as described and just let them go. Try to meditate in the same place each time and more or less at the same time or times of day or night. If your attention drifts do not be concerned, merely bring it back to observing your breathing. It is important not to expect too much of yourself or set yourself specific goals or outcomes.

Progressive muscle relaxation (a choice)

Progressive muscle relaxation is the safest method of relaxation for people with depression to use on their own. If you find that you are unable to focus sufficiently for the body scan or that you need a form of relaxation that is more structured, this form of relaxation when stressed is the one for you. Like any other form of relaxation, this form requires practice to be effective. It takes time to relax stiff muscles, so be patient with yourself.

This is a traditional and successful technique of relaxation developed by Dr Edmund Jacobson in the 1930s. It helps to ease tight muscles, lower blood pressure and slow down an overactive mind. It involves systematic tensing and releasing of the sixteen muscle groups in the body. All you have to do is tense each muscle group vigorously for approximately ten seconds but not hard enough to cause discomfort, and then release for ten to fifteen seconds, saying, "Relax". Enjoy the slack feeling in your muscles and pause for a few seconds before tensing the next muscle group. It's important to concentrate on the sensation of tensing and relaxing as you work through the muscles in your body. If you don't feel relaxed the first time, tense and then relax once or twice more after waiting a few seconds between each phase. Follow these instructions for progressive muscle relaxation.

Find a quiet room and sit in a comfortable chair. Make sure that your back is well supported, that your feet are on the floor and your hands are resting loosely. Now settle back and close your eyes, anticipating the pleasurable feeling of a relaxed body.

1. Start by clenching your fists tightly and then relax, be aware of the tense feeling ... hold ... feel how loose your fists feel now.

2. Bend your elbows and tense your biceps in both arms, be aware of the tension, hold ... then relax your biceps and straighten your arms..

3. Tighten your triceps (muscles under your arms) by extending them, hold and then release.

4. Move to your face and tense your forehead, frown, then raise your eyebrows as high as you can ... hold and then relax.

5. Tighten up all the muscles around your eyelids ... hold and then relax your eyelids.

6. Clench your teeth and tighten your jaw ... hold and then release those muscles and let your jaw hang limply with your lips parted.

7. Tense the muscles in your neck by pulling your head back as hard as comfortable ... relax ... then roll it to the left then to the right and forward ... hold and then relax.

8. Raise your shoulders towards your ears ... hold and then relax.., feel the relaxation spreading through your neck, head and shoulders.

9. Pull your shoulder blades together as if they were touching ... hold and then relax your shoulders.

10. Tighten the muscles in your chest ... suck in some air ... hold and then release them.

11. Pull your stomach muscles in as tightly as possible ... hold and then release them.

12. Tense your lower back muscles by gently arching your back ... hold and then release.

13. Tense your buttock muscles ... hold and then relax them.

14. Squeeze your thigh muscles as far as your knees by pressing down on your heels ... hold and then release them.

15. Flex your toes gently to tighten calf muscles ... hold and relax.

16. Tense your feet by pointing your toes ... hold and then relax them.

17. Progressively tense and then relax all the muscle groups. After that scan your body for remnants of tension. If a particular set of muscles remains uncomfortable, tense and then release them once or twice more, until you feel completely relaxed.

18. Complete your relaxation by imagining a calm, easing wave flowing through your body.

Daily practice

Daily mindfulness usually involves one or two 20 – 40 minutes per day of lying or sitting and meditating. After the first week or two start with 10 minutes and build to 20 minutes over time. Do not expect too much of yourself or push yourself or you will be defeating the object of the meditation. Though some people meditate for very long periods observing the processes of their thoughts and feelings in an atmosphere of quiet, this is not advised without the assistance of a trained person.

The advantages of simply observing

Most of the time there is constant chatter in our mind – anxieties, needs, reminders, feelings and so on. We may not be focussing on specific thoughts, ideas or emotions. With mindfulness meditation you can create a space inside your mind, a greater peacefulness. You can learn to concentrate your attention on specific areas of your thinking, observe them and then make choices about how to respond to them. If they are worrying thoughts you can label them and let them go. All this is possible but it requires discipline and time.

In his book, *The Mindful Brain,* Daniel J Siegel explains how mindfulness can change our physiology and our mental functions so that we develop an enhanced sense of wellbeing, cope better with the stresses of life, react less emotionally and more rationally and become more balanced and objective.

Learning all of this is truly wonderful and worth the effort put into achieving it.

Unleashing emotions through mindfulness training

The experience of emotional pain and suffering as in the case of depression can be changed by the quality of our attention to it. In mild forms of depression, destructive thoughts may be ignored and ease can follow. However if your depression is severe and your mood despairing, too much introspection could increase your emotional pain. For example your interpretations or judgements about the pain, such as, why should this happen to me, what have I done to deserve this. Often the suffering can be worsened by memories or emotions such as anger. This type of feeling and thinking can escalate in spirals out of control.

> If you are severely depressed and your emotions overwhelm you, you may find coping too difficult and even disturbing. At the worst, thoughts might turn to suicide. For these reasons I repeat that delving into deep meditation for severely depressed people without the assistance of a therapist is dangerous.

Healing story: *The Road to Recovery*

Tony was about to open another bottle of gin in an attempt to slow his churning thoughts, when he felt a sudden warm, heaviness on his lap. In his drunken state, he could have sworn that sitting there quite comfortably was a small alien with a pale pointed face. It stared at him with its blue, slanted eyes. He was about to push it away when he heard a deep, steady purr. It was a cat that had crept in through the open window. Looking down at its markings he recognised she was a Siamese; a beauty with an elegant pale lilac-grey body and velvety ears, paws and tail. Tentatively, he placed a hand on her head and stroked her. Her purr deepened and she snuggled up to him. *Don't get too comfortable; you can't stay.*

He asked neighbours if they had lost a cat and put up notices. When he had no response he gave her a temporary home. He became used to her around and when she wasn't claimed after a month, he decided to keep her. The name he gave her was Ally, because he had first thought she was an alien and it was also his name for his beloved dead aunt Alexandra.

Without realising it, Tony began talking to the cat. She responded with a miaow or a throaty purr. Telling her how miserable he felt and how apprehensive he was about leaving the house gave him relief. *It's scary out there. Who knows what awful things could happen to me, I might as well try to make the best of things,* he said to her, opening another bottle. *One more won't hurt, just a little one,* he said, stroking her head. When he'd had too much to drink he'd attempt to explain it away to Ally. *I know I went over the top but I can give it up any time I like and when I'm ready I will, but I need it right now.*

Ally began to make herself at home the way that cats do, by sleeping on his bed as if she owned it, sitting on his lap and cuddling into the soft lounge chairs. She sniffed at the messy papers, greasy plates and empty bottles, lifting her paw in disdain. He muttered excuses to himself and to her but rarely cleaned up. When he was sober they ate in the kitchen together and he fed her tit bits from the table. With Ally on his lap, he stroked her velvety fur and was more at peace.

Ally spent most of her day sleeping in warm spots and towards evening she usually had one of her crazy spells when she'd climb curtains or go dashing across the room and back. He was boiling the kettle for coffee, when Ally jumped into one of the high kitchen cupboards. He heard the clink of breaking china and seconds later, Ally leapt down on the floor with a howl, furiously licking her bleeding paw. He felt her all over and she seemed unhurt apart from a badly cut paw. She was bleeding heavily and after gently bandaging her paw, he placed her in a cardboard box with a cushion at the bottom and left for the vet. As expected, she needed stitches. Some of the week's drinking money went to the vet, and there would be at least another consultation to check her progress. Ally had become so much part of his life, that he couldn't bear the idea of her being in pain.

A few weeks later the cat's paw healed and she was as active as usual. Around this time, Tony received a letter from his wife seeking a divorce. They had been separated for a few years but he had hoped for reconciliation. Her cold, matter-of-fact approach upset him and he drank to numb the pain of his longing for what might have been. In a semi-stupor, he forgot to feed Ally or leave her water.

When he recovered he looked for Ally in all her hiding places – the linen basket, behind the curtain and under the doona, but she had gone. He desperately wanted her back but there was no sign of her. After days of searching he gave up, thinking he'd never see her again. He blamed himself. *If I hadn't been drunk and if I'd looked after her properly this wouldn't have happened. I've pushed everyone I care for away – my wife, my friends and now Ally. It's all my fault.*

He punished himself by not touching a drink for a day but had to spend the next one in bed. He vomited and shook so uncontrollably that he had to have a few beers to settle himself down. He made one more attempt at giving up alcohol but the identical symptoms made him realise he was locked into a cycle he couldn't break.

Weeks later he was relaxing in his easy chair when he felt a familiar heaviness in his lap. Ally was back. She was thin, her formerly shiny coat dull and matted. He opened a tin of her favourite, tuna casserole and she ate hungrily. Later, while he stroked and petted her he made up his mind to stop procrastinating. *It's time I looked after both of us. I'm no good to you or anyone else if I carry on drinking but I can't give up the booze on my own. I have to ask for help.*

A local doctor booked him into a detox centre where his addiction was treated. Before he left he put Ally into a cattery. This time he wouldn't take the chance of losing her. The period of withdrawal was awful. The physical cravings, the restlessness and the way he hurt all over made him hate alcohol and despise his weakness.

He returned from his ordeal drained, his legs like jelly. Without the blunting of alcohol, his emotions were easily stirred and unpredictable. Feelings of panic and a deep aching despair filled him and he longed for a drink to dull it. He was in trouble and he knew he had to seek further help from his doctor. If he didn't have treatment for his fears and depression, his intention to stay sober wouldn't last. His doctor gave him calming medication and recommended he attend an Alcoholics Anonymous group.

It's time for more human help, he said stroking the cat. And so Tony continued his long and difficult journey along the road to recovery.

EIGHTEEN
✿

MINDFULNESS AS PART OF DAILY LIFE

Though meditation is the most common and direct way of learning to live in the moment and the method taught to practice the mindfulness technique, it may not suit everyone's needs. For those people, the practice of mindfulness in their daily lives can become a method of being in touch with their current experience. The method can be used every day and in most situations, to remain in touch with current experiences.

We all have the capacity to be calmer and more balanced and mindfulness techniques help us to attain this. As mentioned previously, mindfulness is particularly helpful when your mind is bombarded with negative thoughts, stuck on hurtful repetitive ideas, or if you keep replaying negative scenes. In whatever manner you decide to practice, these are a few simple tips to help you on your way.

Using mindfulness in your daily life

Mindful eating

Sit down at a table to eat your meal without the distraction of television, phones, books newspapers, magazines or talking. As always take deep breaths before you start to eat. Then let all other thoughts go as you take one bit of food at a time, cut the food if it is necessary. Then notice how your arm lifts the fork as you secure it, take it to your mouth. Place the food past your lips slowly and taste it, noticing the taste and texture. Chew it slowly. Continue staying in the here and now as you eat the remainder of your meal in this way. Not only is less food filling but the slow chewing is an excellent aid to digestion.

Taking a mindful walk

Remember your deep breaths and as you walk be aware of the muscles in each leg and foot stepping forward touching the ground, heavily or lightly. Is your pace fast or slow, rhythmical or not? Be aware whether the ground is hard or soft. Notice how you hold your hands and head as you walk. You are in the present and you have no other thoughts. You look at nature, the shape and colour of trees and leaves that mark the season, the sky and the ground. You are aware of tiny details like flowers and grasses that you have missed before. You feel the sun or the wind and hear your feet engage with the earth. There are other noises too – of birds or branches swaying or people talking. You notice all animals, houses and people as you continue your walk.

Red light meditation

At a red light use that waiting time to notice how your body feels in the car, how you sit on the seat, touch the wheel and notice your feet touch the carpet floor. Take your big breaths and staying very alert with eyes open, keep breathing comfortably as you prepare to move off focusing on the traffic and on safety while driving.

Household chores and gardening

You can apply the same principles as before to whatever you are doing, observing and not judging, in the present without being distracted by thoughts.

With all of these daily activities being mindful allows you to be calmer and more focussed. When you first practice mindfulness on a daily basis, it is best to start with one particular activity for example, gardening. Once you are successful at mindfully gardening or doing household chores, you can then include other aspects of your daily life. However far you wish to take mindfulness training you will appreciate the calm it can give you.

The following table analyses mindfulness or lack of it during a person's daily activities.

MINDFULNESS DAILY ACTIVITIES TABLE

Situation	Activity	Thoughts	Emotion	Orientation	Observations	Action	Emotion
Kitchen.	Eating breakfast.	I must hurry up. I'm late for work. I was late all week – will get into trouble.	Anxiety.	In the past.	Don't notice much – food tastes good.	Left for work before I finished ironing my shirt properly.	Stressed
The next day: Kitchen.	Eating breakfast.	I'm going to take my time today.	Relaxed.	In the present.	Notice muscle movement as I cut my food and lift it to my mouth; the texture of the food. Chew slowly and taste food. Each bit is different.	Finish a delicious breakfast.	Relaxed
Outside.	Walking.	I used to walk with dad down this street.	Sad and tense.	In the past.	Jerky steps, slow pace.	Hurry the walk.	Unhappy.
The next day: Outside.	Walking.	Enjoying the sunshine, trees and flowers, birds.	Relaxed.	Present.	Easy, rhythmical pace.	Take my time.	Relaxed and peaceful.

NINETEEN

RELATING TO OTHERS WITH MINDFUL COMPASSION

Depression can be cruel

One of the cruellest aspects of depression is the emptiness or woodenness that strikes with most severe depression. Withdrawal from friends and loved ones occurs frequently so that you can feel disconnected from a once-loved partner and previously close friends. The shift that takes place when depression strikes, makes it difficult to remember the love once felt and reciprocated. You may even find difficulty remembering feeling love and care and conclude it wasn't real and create a dark cloud around all your relationships. Consequently, you might find yourself becoming critical of everyone in your life. Suffering, irritability and lack of sleep can impair or distort your judgement and you withdraw further. Depression also affects your view of yourself, so that your self-esteem disintegrates, guilt may surface and you tend to beat up on yourself. And at times it may seem as if you are alone in your suffering.

Compassion

As well as the key concepts of awareness and acceptance of our experience, thoughts and feelings, we need to turn to another important area, compassion. Compassion not only means accepting and acknowledging the fact of universal suffering, but in addition, having concern for another person's difficulties, their suffering or pain. Compassion requires you to understand what it is like to be in that person's predicament or suffering by "standing in their shoes." It implies empathy with another person but not being involved in their suffering.

Nor does it mean that another person should take advantage of you or your kindness and act towards you in a destructive manner.

Feeling for others who are in pain is a step forward for a person who is depressed and trapped in their self-hurt.

You will be able to relate to others by accepting their qualities and flaws and having realistic expectations. Your emotional space for others in your life will expand and relationships with loved ones will eventually become more trusting and closer. It might feel as if a light or warmth has been turned on when you want to smile at someone or put an arm around them.

COMPASSION FOR OTHERS

Situation	Activity	Other person	Realise their difficulty	Emotion	Action	Feeling
Outside.	Walking.	See an old man.	He walks slowly, head down.	I feel for him. He looks very unhappy.	I smile and nod. He nods back.	I feel good.
At a meeting.	Listening to speaker.	The woman next to me is shaking and looks worried.	Holds paper in her hand. She whispers that she speaks next and is very scared.	I imagine how nervous she is.	I quietly tell her to imagine she's talking to me.	She does well and I feel good.
In the town.	Shopping.	A teenager bumps into me.	See her frightened look and sad eyes.	Feel concern. Something is wrong	I smile at her. She continues walking.	I am still concerned about her.
In the garden.	Cutting roses.	See the woman next door.	She told me earlier that she is very ill. She looks dreadful	I feel concerned for her.	I go up to the fence to ask how she is feeling.	Concerned. I will visit her tomorrow.

Self-compassion

Self-compassion is a cornerstone of the mindfulness approach. However it is difficult for many depressed people to be kind and understanding to themselves and avoid self-criticism and judgement.

Self-compassion is not selfishness, egocentrism or self-pity. Being self-compassionate means seeing things in perspective – acknowledging that you are suffering while others might be suffering even more.

The most important aspect of self-compassion is love, accepting, supporting and believing in yourself. It implies being gentle and kind to yourself and yet being aware of your strengths and limitations. You can gradually learn to love yourself mindfully in the following way:

- Being kind and gentle to yourself every day.

- Becoming aware of your own needs and attempting to satisfy them as you do other's needs.

- Looking after your body as regards the food you eat, exercising and getting enough sleep.

- Looking after your mind so that you remain challenged and stimulated.

- Not allowing yourself to be used or manipulated by others.

- Expressing any talents and skills you may have, especially creative talent.

- Treating yourself as you would others-with respect and kindness.

- Use affirmations such as:

    - I care about myself.

    - I am important to myself and others.

    - I am gentle with myself.

    - Today is a day for valuing everything I do.

    - Today is a day for not judging myself so harshly.

    - I will leave perfectionism at home when I go to work.

- ◆ Now create your own suitable affirmations that will add to your sense of self-compassion.
- Fighting against your expectations of outcomes.
- Finding the time for your daily meditation.

Healing story: *Letting go*

Karen rode passed all the houses in her suburb and was heading for open land. Peddling fast she was enjoying her bicycle ride more than she had enjoyed anything lately. She had left the house after an unsatisfying morning painting. The canvass had looked dull, lacking the strength and vitality of her earlier work. Painting usually lifted her mood, fired her imagination, but this time it was not working for her.

When the bike suddenly reared up and then shuddered to a stop she was nearly thrown off. She had a flat, front tyre. A feel in her pockets revealed no phone. It was still on the table next to her bed. After wheeling the bike back along the road, she sat exhausted at the roadside hoping for help. No one stopped or even slowed down until a woman crossed the road. She was slight and tanned, her skin glowing in the afternoon light. She introduced herself as Erin and offered her help. "I live in one of the caravans near here." She pointed to a clump of trees. "I'm sure one of the guys will fix it for you."

They wheeled the bike down a dirt path to the caravans parked under shade near the trickle of a stream. Erin's caravan was small and richly decorated with swirls of colour. While a young man repaired the tyre, they had tea and biscuits. Karen sighed, overcome with tiredness. *I shouldn't have come out today...and certainly not as far from home as this,* she thought.

Erin had been watching Karen and hesitated before speaking. "Are you ok?"

"I'll be fine," Karen answered quickly, attempting a smile.

After a few moments of silence Erin looked directly at her. "My cousin in the next caravan is a psychic...a healer...perhaps she could help you."

"Thank you...but I'll be fine," Karen replied a little hesitantly.

She had heard about psychic claims and felt uncertain and Erin was a stranger. But by the time she had finished drinking her tea, she felt so flat and wrung out that she was prepared to try anything.

A musky smell of incense and cigarettes swamped the interior of the psychic's caravan. Before her stood an imposing woman. Karen sat on a velvety chair while the woman hummed softly to herself. A glimmering crystal ball on the table dominated.

Karen felt uneasy. *I shouldn't have agreed to this. Heaven knows what's going to happen.*

"Watch the ball and concentrate on it," the woman said softly.

As Karen felt herself drift, the woman's voice reached her from further and further away.

Later, the woman offered her insights. "My crystal ball tells me that you are going through a difficult time but have learnt much and that soon you will move in the direction of the third and most important phase of a woman's life, the wise woman phase. The first phase was at thirteen, the second was your mature childbearing phase and now you are about to enter the wise woman phase."

Karen shrugged unimpressed. There was nothing new in what she was told.

"While you move towards maturity and greater understanding, there is a part of you that is still afraid and vulnerable and pulls you back," the psychic said. "That part takes the form of a small girl who feels unloved. The girl has searched all her life for love and has done all that was expected of her to prove that she was worthy of loving. She needs you to acknowledge her. Only you can make her feel cared for and understand what she needs. It is you who can comfort her and let her know that she has always done her best. Encourage her to let go of the restraints that prevent her from becoming that wise woman. Encourage her to love herself."

Karen sat up in the chair.

The psychic didn't wait for her response and took a draw of her cigarette. "I predict that you will find that you have learnt much from your present emotional upheaval. This, together with all your lifetime experiences, will prepare you for your new state of honour. You'll be regarded as a knowledgeable one, a teacher and comforter in the ways of life. You will listen to your intuition and trust your judgment as never before."

Karen began to speak but the woman held up her hand to still her. She looked into the crystal ball and said, "As you travel and explore, you will soon discover yourself. This then, shall be the most satisfying time of your life." The woman rubbed her hands, looked at Karen and pushed a saucer towards her for payment.

Karen smiled, thinking she had heard some of the predictions before or read them in magazines.

In spite of her cynicism, Karen felt stronger. Her bicycle was mended and after thanking everyone, she rode off quickly taking the scenic route home through the forest. She peddled through the lush greenery, listening to the soothing hum of insects and birdcalls. Here and there she stopped to admire a plant or a tree, wishing she had her sketch pad and pastels with her to capture her own view of the beauty surrounding her. Deep in the forest, she came across a pool of water, almost hidden by flowering bushes. Edged with lacy ferns, it was clear and sparkling. The day was warm and the water so inviting that she stripped and waded into the pool. Floating like an exotic flower, only the ripples from her slight movements disturbed the smooth surface. When she reluctantly stepped out of the pool and dried herself in the warm air, she noticed her reflection in the mirrored surface. At first, she saw herself as a young girl, smiling mischievously, slipping into the water like a seal. Then her adult self appeared. She looked at an unsmiling image of herself with her father's critical eyes and recoiled from it. Daring to look again, she held her breath at the attractive face, shining eyes, and well-proportioned body. This time she liked what she saw – an earthy nude as ripe and plump as a peach.

Her curly hair dried in the sun and it flowed freely, cascading over her shoulders. A new optimism surged through her.

PART 5

HARMONY AND BALANCE

TWENTY
※

FINDING STRENGTH WITHIN

Intuition

Much has been said about negativity and little about the healing, positive side of thinking and feeling. Often one tends to forget that we all have an inner voice that can guide and support us in times of uncertainty and despondency. Just as you have a reservoir of destructive automatic thoughts buried in your mind that has developed over time, you also have positive thoughts, ideas and feelings available to help you.

Intuition is that inner voice, an inner knowing or flash of insight. It is a feeling in your heart or gut, a realisation from deep inside that guides you to possibilities in the world around you. Some call it a spiritual feeling and others call it divine help. In part, it emanates from the source of your wisdom seated in the database of your unconscious. The data base records knowledge and experience you have gained since early childhood. Intuition is the potent carrier of insight that opens new vistas for you.

If you keep an open mind and are honest with yourself, it will be easier to be in touch with your intuition. How many times have you known that something felt right, while others have disagreed? Used to thinking negatively, you may have turned your back on your flash of insight or failed to give it the attention it deserved.

Have you ever been disturbed by a sense of foreboding, an inner warning about a future occurrence or felt unsure about someone or a particular situation? Most of us have experienced this inner knowing, but not all of us take it seriously or act on it.

Carl Jung, famous psychoanalyst and contemporary of Sigmund Freud, described intuition as one of the ways in which we orientate ourselves to our world. In *Psychological Types,* Jung defined intuition as "... a perception of realities which are not known to consciousness, and which goes via the unconscious ... it is an active creative process which seizes on the situation and tries to alter it according to its vision. It has the capacity to inspire, and in every hopelessly blocked situation [it] works automatically towards the issue which no other function could discover. Whenever a judgment or diagnosis has to be made, in the dark intuition comes into play. Scientists and physicians, judges and generals all must make use of this faculty at times, and of course ordinary people as well."

If your inner voice is blocked

Depression can dampen your inner voice. In a down mood you may tell yourself that you're not an intuitive person and that you never hear an inner voice or have a gut feeling about things. How then can you access that intuitive part of yourself if it seems blocked, lost or hidden? Try to think back to a time when you rescued yourself from a difficult situation or managed to avoid something going wrong in your life. Have you ever wondered how you managed to do that? At the time, you may have dismissed it, as depressed people often do, and thought only of the negatives again. Whether you believe that it was spiritual intervention, luck or your own intuition that helped you on those occasions, is your interpretation.

What you do need to realise is that you have a positive side that is geared towards your survival and growth as a human being.

Tune into your intuition

If you listen to what your heart is telling you, you'll feel a sense of "knowing" that you're on the right track. You'll feel a "rightness" in your body – a resonance within. If you are unsure of your direction, or feel confused about the signals you are receiving, then wait. The answers will come to you later, in a dream or possibly a daydream.

If you have been depressed for a long time, the negativity of your thinking and moments of dejection may have blunted your ease in connecting with your inner feelings. Realise that intuition is like a fragile butterfly and its wings can be easily crushed in a destructive environment. Be patient with yourself, don't push too hard for that inner response. Intuition flourishes in a calm, open atmosphere.

Practise listening for intuitive messages and jot them down when you notice them. Remember that there may be a negative thought on the ready to attack that new creative idea.

Case study

Shaun, aged nineteen, had been depressed for almost two years. There had been a few lighter and more optimistic days but depression and insecurity prevented him from making plans for his future. Though he had hoped for a career in engineering, each time he thought of enrolling at the university his fears and negative thoughts swamped his progress. *I'll never get there...I'll muck things up...I'll never be good enough*, he'd say to himself. When friends tried to encourage him, he'd look away and shake his head. He continued struggling with his fears for months and did nothing to secure his future.

One summer there was so much rain that the drains blocked and water seeped into the house. He had been warning his father for ages that something had to be done about the drains. Instead of saying *I told you so*, he applied himself to unblocking the drains. Once the danger of flooding was under control, he looked for the builder's plans and examined all the drains. He needed to design a system that would ensure drainage in future and spent hours at his drawing board until he had designed a workable system. Finally he worked with a plumber until a better system was satisfactorily installed.

The gratitude and admiration of his father and the rest of his family finally convinced him to follow his path and finally he enrolled at the university engineering faculty.

Gradually his depression lifted and though he struggled with the load of work, he became an excellent student.

Balancing your intuition

Intuition needs to be backed up by truth, an open mind and an ability to face reality.

There are times when your intuition may tell you something unpleasant or hurtful such as, your lover is cheating on you or that a friend is talking about you behind your back. How do you know that these feelings that appear to come from within are true. They may be distortions of fact or represent your fears or jealousies. Many other factors could be influencing you at the time as well, such as your mood, time of day or information from others. *That's why it's essential to check out your intuitions with fact.* You may need to ask people whose opinions you value, compare and weigh them up, do your own research or ask an authority to be certain. Never make important decisions on gut feeling alone. Therefore, intuition may be a powerful pointer in a specific direction but not always the entire truth.

New ways of thinking

Expectations of others and learned beliefs from parents or teachers may have influenced your thinking and stifled your intuition and insight. In this example a young woman longed to play the violin. A teacher once told her that she had no musical talent but she sensed this as incorrect. She felt rhythm within and taught herself to play the guitar. However, she had a family to care for and a full-time job. Unless she followed that inner light, her hopes of playing the violin would come to nothing. As she desperately wanted to learn to play the violin, she found a way to fit it into her busy schedule by going for lessons on the weekend.

Experimenting with new ideas

As depression can result in low self-esteem, reduced energy and motivation, the idea of experimenting with intuition may not appeal to you at first. Approach these new ideas slowly and imagine that they are like a buffet of delicious food presented on a table for your pleasure. Pick those tasty morsels that appeal to you most. As you become a little more adventurous, choose something new that interests you.

Try not to close your mind to the idea of creative involvement, think of a few things you enjoyed before you became depressed. Perhaps you could try them again. Always tackle the least threatening and simplest activity first. You may have enjoyed going for a walk in the past. This is something you can do with a friend. If you enjoy it, go again until you have the confidence to try another activity. In this way you can build up your confidence and gradually reintroduce more of the things that gave you pleasure in the past. Eventually your ideas will flow freely and more creatively.

Dreams and intuition

Always have a pen and note pad next to your bed. Dreams are easily forgotten unless you make the effort to recall them. Recalling your dreams becomes easier in time as you practise.

Before going to sleep, read the account of your dreams for the previous night so that you can connect with them. As you fall asleep tell yourself that you will remember your dream. When you wake up write down all you can recall about your dream plus details of how you felt during the dream – happy, afraid, sad. Note any associations to the dream such as your activities during the day or your feelings when you went to sleep. Have a light or torch next to your bed so that you can record a dream if you wake during the night or early morning. Don't try and probe your dream for meaning, just write down the content and associations. Also make a note of any fantasies you have during that day.

Your feelings, dreams and daydreams aim to alert you to what your mind is telling you. You could call this an internal message system. Use of a journal will provide you with the opportunity to note inner information received daily through your emotions, dreams and fantasies.

When to consult a professional therapist

The unconscious mind is intricate and often confusing because of its symbolic nature. Therefore, analysis of frightening, negative or recurring dreams is best left to the experts. This is not an area to experiment with or attempt to unravel with pop psychology. If you want to delve into that deeper world consult a psychologist or a psychotherapist.

At depression's lowest point you may find difficulty in thinking of any positives in your past or be unable to relate to once functioning aspects of yourself that now seem lost or disconnected. Your daydreams and dreams may be destructive and even harmful. When you are depressed, negatives seem to colour the future black and frightening.

Unfortunately some depressed people have memories of hurtful or even traumatic childhood experiences that dominate their thinking. If you are plagued by memories of the past, a skilled psychologist can assist you in lifting this black veil.

Healing story: *Family treasures*

Sara was nineteen when she married Matthew in a country church. Shortly after their simple reception, her father kissed her and handed her a gift of a small red leather box. "We are not wealthy people but your mother and I are giving you a few of our family treasures, so that part of our history will always be with you to pass onto your children." Sara thanked him and put the box in her overnight case.

Matthew was ambitious for wealth and success and believed their future lay in the city. Although Sara preferred farm life, she loved Matthew and was prepared to move to please him. Shortly after the reception the couple said goodbye to their relatives. Leaving immediately was the only way Sara could cope with the pain of parting from her family. They took a taxi to the airport.

She knew she had to sever her emotional ties with home and concentrate on the adventure ahead. After she had wiped away her tears, she took Matthew's hand and relaxed as well as she could in the uncomfortable seat. When she woke from a short sleep she thought of her parents' gift. Curious about its contents she opened her overnight case and ran her finger tips over the fine leather box with its scrolled pattern. Against the silk lining of the lid was a familiar photograph of her parents and sister. Beneath it was a delicate silk scarf with a sprig of blue flowers that had belonged to her grandmother. Sara held the scarf to her lips, remembering her grandmother's blue eyes sparkling when she wore it on special occasions. There was a silver teaspoon with a decorative handle that had belonged to her great grandmother. Her mother used it only for visitors. She found a tortoiseshell comb inlaid with mother of pearl next. Her great aunt Bessie had inherited it from her grandmother and wore it with pride in her long hair. The comb brought back fond memories of family gatherings and the fun she once had playing with her cousins. Tucked into one corner of the box was a black velvet pouch and in it were three gold coins. In the other corner was a small blue case containing a silver brooch in the form of a dove with shimmering wings and an eye made from a glinting green stone. Her mother had told her it had been a wedding gift to her great-grandmother from her beloved cousin, whom she had been forbidden to marry. She replaced the contents of the box and put it in her handbag.

Within a few days Sara and Matthew realised that living in the city would be more difficult than they had imagined. Food was far more expensive than it had been during their visit a year earlier. They found a boarding house with cheap rent and searched for work. In the first few weeks, neither found the jobs they wanted. They realised that they would have to accept whatever was offered. When the money they had saved dwindled, Sara thought of the gold coins. She sold one coin and it bought them food for almost a week. While Matthew continued looking for a job, Sara managed to find work as a hotel cleaning maid. Her salary did not cover the rent and so she sold another coin.

They were on the point of returning home when Matthew had a lucky break. He came across a carpenter who had a furniture stall in the city. Matthew complimented him on the quality of his work. Flattered, the carpenter offered to try him out as an apprentice. While they waited for Mathew's pay they spent the last gold coin. Matthew devoted himself to his work and in a short time found that he had a talent for carpentry. They moved into a bed-sitter and made it as comfortable as they could with bits and pieces found at markets and their wedding gifts. Once Matthew had served his apprenticeship, he sold his furniture at fairs and markets.

Meantime Sara had become a receptionist. She enjoyed her work and the company of her work mates. When her closest friend at work married, she gave her great aunt Bessie's tortoiseshell comb as a present. Around this time Sara fell pregnant and left her job. When the baby was born they called him James after Matthew's father. Sara wasn't a natural mother and resented her crying, demanding baby. James exhausted her and she longed for a little time to herself. A neighbour loved children and offered to care for him for a few hours each week. In gratitude, Sara impulsively opened the red box and gave the kind woman her grandmother's silk scarf.

When James was five, she thought of returning to work but she fell pregnant with Paul. After Paul was weaned he went off his appetite. Sara remembered the decorative, spoon in the red box. He was attracted to its colourful handle and readily ate from it. From then on she kept the spoon in the kitchen to mix his vegetables and fed him with it.

Matthew's furniture sold for a good price and the couple eventually bought a modest house and Sara was able to give up her job. Once they settled, Sara tossed the red leather box in a top cupboard. Their lives should have been easier, but instead of drawing them together the two children were a wall between them. They hardly spent time alone and when they did, Sara was usually tired and irritable from caring for the children all day. Matthew had difficulty coping with her moodiness and instead of supporting her, withdrew, throwing himself into his work. Though she fought to remain positive, she eventually succumbed to a crushing depression.

In the first year after leaving home, she had kept in touch with her parents and sister by letter and the occasional phone call. As the months passed, she found less and less time to write to them and their conversations gradually became forced. Her father was almost fifty and her mother was in her early forties when she was born and the age difference between them had always been a barrier to their closeness. She had been away five years, when her father died suddenly but she decided not to attend the funeral. Four years later, her mother died but instead of listening to her inner voice that urged her home, she used the excuse that Paul was too young to leave at home and that travelling with him would be too difficult. Her sporadic correspondence with her sister ceased as well and cut her off from her family and her past.

Sara had the home she had always dreamed of but she was dissatisfied – a housewife alone caring for her children and she longed to be back in the workforce. Waves of despair surrounded her, and her lack of direction sent her into panic. She began to relive her memories and fantasise about her youth. As she opened the window of the past, she longed for the love and security her parents had given her. One evening she was thinking about her family when she remembered the red leather box. She blamed herself for being careless with the precious gift. All she had left to pass onto her children was the family photograph and the dove brooch. She wept with guilt for breaking the bond with her parents and failing to keep in contact with her sister. It was time to listen to her feelings instead of trying to escape from them. She found a gold frame for the photograph and placed it on her bedside table. Then she turned to the blue satin case. The silver brooch was tarnished but intact. She cleaned it until it shone and its bejewelled eye twinkled. Pinning it on her shirt, she admired it in the mirror. She thought about her parents' gift and realised that what they had given her was a message about the importance of family ties. It was her link with the past but she had not valued it. In her race to establish a new life in the city with Matthew, she had cut her ties with the past and in doing so lost part of herself.

A few months later her inner voice told her to visit her old home and her parents' graves. She also contacted her sister and arranged to meet her. She was learning that her inner voice was the one thing she could rely on.

TWENTY-ONE

DEVELOPING HARMONY AND BALANCE

Encouraging your energy balance

There are a number of disciplines, mainly originating from Asia that emphasise the development of harmony and balance and the release of energy or the life force. The Japanese call it "ki", the Chinese know it as "chi" and in India it's called "prana". The belief is that energy should flow freely and that blockages and restrictions will ultimately lead to emotional and physical illness.

The following disciplines emphasise harmony, cohesiveness and balance. Although none of them can be said to cure depression, they encourage relaxation, and provide an environment conducive to peace and recovery. If used together with medications and counselling, they may provide a well-rounded approach for *mild depression.*

Tai Chi

Millions of Chinese and other people throughout the world practise this ancient form of moving meditation, which aims to integrate body and mind. Its slow but disciplined positions teach you gracefulness and serenity, while strengthening your body and encouraging the flow of energy channels.

Yoga

Yoga focuses on unifying body and mind. It offers more than stretching exercises. It is well known for its philosophy and ethics of life, diet, breath control, methods of concentrating and meditation. The practice of yoga is thought to reduce the incidence of chronic illness and stress.

Acupuncture

Energy is believed to flow in meridians or channels in your body and if it is restricted or excessive, poor emotional and physical health will follow. To return you to a state of balance and wellbeing, the acupuncturist inserts needles into specific points along meridians for about thirty minutes.

Massage

Massage refers to a group of disciplines where pressure and friction are applied to your muscles and joints. There are several different massage therapies which attempt to promote physical integration in different ways. Some of them are:

- Shiatsu – massage of pressure points aims to release blocked energies and restore harmony.

- Swedish massage – strokes and friction applied during the massage are intended to reduce pain or emotional stress.

- Reflexology – a technique for specific zones or reflexes of your hands and feet, believed to correspond to parts of the body. Massage of the zones returns the body to a state of harmony and health.

Reiki

Treatments follow a traditional pattern of healing through placing hands on or over the body in different positions. Reiki is also about the release and balance of energy and is believed to bring about relaxation and healing.

Kinesiology

Kinesiology is the practice of muscle testing to determine imbalances of mind and body. The practitioner places your body in specific positions and then applies light pressure. According to the response, pressures and imbalances in your body and nervous system are identified and appropriate treatment determined. Treatments include gentle massage, attention to food sensitivities, vitamin and mineral deficiencies and imbalances. Bach flower remedies and other homeopathic remedies are used as energy harmonising techniques.

Emotional Freedom Technique (EFT)

EFT is a form of "emotional" acupuncture that uses the meridians based on acupuncture without the use of needles or pressure point massage. The specific points are tapped with fingertips or finger pads while a specific worrying problem or traumatic event is thought about. In addition positive affirmations or statements are made. It is important to tap the correct area and use fingertips or pads in the right way. The fingertips of the index and middle fingers are used. All hand jewellery such as watches, rings and bracelets must be removed.

The correct tapping points

- The top of the head – at the centre of the skull (using both hands).
- Eyebrow – just above and to the side of the nose (using a hand for each eye).
- Edge of the eye – on the bone above the outside corner of the eye (using a hand for each eye).
- Under the eye – two centimetres below the pupil (using a hand on each side).
- Under the nose – in the crease between nose and mouth.
- Chin – the middle of the chin below the mouth.
- Collarbone – the point where the breastbone and the first rib meet (using a hand on each side).
- Under the arm – on the side, even with the nipple or about 10 centimetres below the armpit (using a hand on each side).
- Wrists – the inside of each wrist.

Colour Therapy

Colour as a therapy is a non-invasive therapy dating back thousands of years and thought to have been used in ancient India, China and Egypt. Colour is light of varying wavelengths and its energy is employed in Colour Therapy. The different frequencies of light in colours are used to produce a healing effect.

Healing story: *The suit*

There was once a very old man, leathery and wrinkled with a sharp memory. In spite of his aches and pains, he was happy. Storytelling came to him naturally and he continued to captivate an audience with his tales of wars, famines and great struggles. The story he enjoyed telling most often was about his battle to overcome painful memories of his past.

"On my twenty-first birthday my parents bought me a navy blue, pin-striped suit for a present. It was made of fine wool and designed by the best tailors but I disliked it from the moment I opened the box. When I tried the suit on, it fitted perfectly but it was far too formal. I preferred casual clothing. I put it at the back of my cupboard and forgot about it.

As I tell you about the years that led up to that birthday, you'll understand how the striped suit assumed importance. I had a wonderful childhood, playing games after school and riding my bike with my friends in the streets. My parents weren't the affectionate sort but cared for me well enough and I never went hungry.

Shortly after I turned thirteen my life changed. What happened to me at thirteen, you may ask. Well, my uncle, my mother's brother, crept up to my bedroom one night and slipped into my bed. You can imagine the rest so there's no point going into the horrible details, except to say that I screamed for help but nobody came. I couldn't understand why my favourite uncle I loved so much could do something that awful to me...and not only once. Of course, my parents didn't believe me when I told them what had happened. My father threatened me with a hiding if I didn't cut out the lies. For a long time they wouldn't accept what I had to say, but later, much later, when one of my cousins had a similar visit in the night, they changed their tune. Maybe they felt bad about ignoring my story and that's why they gave me such an expensive present years later.

From being a fun-loving person with lots of friends I turned into a withdrawn, sad one, trusting no one. My school results plummeted and I was dumped from the football team. I was dead inside – no longer laughed or cried. I reckoned that if I couldn't feel, I wouldn't have to remember. Later, when I was working, I didn't date or go to the football either and on weekends I sat around the house.

A few months after my twenty-first birthday, an old bloke joined our company. He sat next to me and talked a lot about his life and his terrible recollections of the war. I didn't say much, just listened. He had been to one of those head doctors who helped him to overcome his nightmares. The doc told him to let his memories of shooting, killing and dying into his dreams ...in little bits at a time. All I know is that he got rid of most of the dark stuff worrying him. I thought a lot about him, and though completely different, compared his story to mine. I reckoned it was time for me to change too, but I had no idea where to start.

The changes in me began with the weirdest dreams. It's hard to believe it but I dreamt about that navy suit at least once a week that year. The first dream about the suit is still sharp. I took it out of the cupboard, shook the dust from it and hung it up to air. My dreams altered when I tried to unpick the still new and stitched pockets. I woke screaming and in a sweat after what I saw in the pockets – snippets from the abuse by my uncle. That dream continued for months until I could look into the pockets without flinching. I didn't dare dream about putting my hand in them until much later.

A year later, I was promoted at work and invited to the company's Christmas dinner. I had only one good suit, the navy one. The most peculiar thing happened when I tried it on the night before the dinner. I hadn't put on an ounce of weight or changed in any way and I suppose it must have fitted, but it felt tight and uncomfortable. The sleeves and legs seemed short. It was probably my imagination. There was nothing wrong with the suit and it wasn't that I cared how it looked, I just knew I couldn't wear it. Luckily, I was able to hire a suit in time for the occasion.

I had gained confidence in my job by then and my dreams about the suit changed. I recall dreaming about trying to rub the pin stripes out of the material. It was a huge job but each time I dreamed, I got rid of a few more stripes. It must have taken ages but when they were all gone, in my dreams, I woke feeling freer.

Around that time, I dated a woman from work but it fizzled out. It was all my fault; I couldn't handle the intimacy side – not with my past. After that I took a long break from women.

Did I tell you about my drinking? It began slowly – a few beers after work or with my meal. When I had to nip out to the hotel for a drink every lunchtime, I knew I was in trouble. It became expensive but I didn't spend on anything else, so I could afford my habit. Most of the men in my family were drunks but that didn't excuse it. I had to give up the booze. I didn't have an option. Luckily, my doctor gave me some tablets to help me over the withdrawal period. It was tough having the shakes, feeling irritable and jumpy and I couldn't go back to work for weeks. For no reason I'd get resentful or very sad and want to cry, then I'd battle for hours to calm down. It felt as if a painful oozing wound inside had opened. My suit dreams at the time were bizarre. The navy material was pulled in all directions and wound itself into knots, white heat escaped from the suit and then the seams burst.

I managed to stay off the booze and knew I couldn't touch as much as a drop or I'd start drinking again. After that my life went along quietly enough for a time and I became aware of small pleasures – a long, hot shower after football, a full moon and stars, a rainbow, walking in the rain, listening to music. I was like a kid again.

It must've been around that time that I worked up the courage to visit my uncle. I told the old bastard what I thought of him and about the damage he'd done to me. Do you know, he didn't have a clue about it. He drank a lot at the time and I worked out that he must have had a few that night. We talked and he apologised, offering to make it up to me, but he didn't know how other than through money. It was amazing how that talk lifted an enormous burden from me. There'd be times when I'd think about it but the painful sting had gone from my memory.

I bet you want to know what happened to the real suit. Well, other than being old-fashioned, it stayed the same, stripes and all. In my life, I was moving ahead. After the meeting with my uncle I went through a growth spurt. I was in my forties, so it was about time it happened. I started dating again and problems to do with sex reared their head but my wife-to-be, Nancy, helped me sort it out. It's a long story and too embarrassing to go into details. Once we were married we made friends with other couples and our life together was happy.

Every now and again I'd have a suit dream. I'd turn out the pockets, throwaway the contents and clean the bits of lint that collected in the trouser turn-ups. The dreams no longer worried me. I smiled to myself when I woke from them. I was doing a bit of inner cleaning, that's all.

The last suit dream I had was in my late fifties, and I remember it clearly. The buttons glowed, fell off and then melted. After that dream I took the suit out of the cupboard. It was still in good condition but I decided it was time to give it to charity. I must tell you, I was pleased to get rid of it and after that and I was at peace."

TWENTY-TWO
✿

KEEPING YOUR BODY IN TUNE

NUTRITION

Many depressed people have a poor appetite and do not eat well. A weak, poorly nourished person will find coming to terms with depression extremely difficult. Eating sandwiches, junk food or left-over scraps unfortunately makes up the inadequate diet of many depressed people who live alone. If you don't feel like eating, try to maintain your strength with small amounts of nutritious food, such as energy shakes, home-made soup, fruit, vegetables and small amounts of protein.

Diet fads

Our newspapers and magazines and television regularly suggest new diets and healthier ways of eating. Though you can't take all the new tips and advice seriously, there are some solid, common-sense approaches to nutrition that are generally well regarded. As always, a balanced diet is best. Complex carbohydrates, a reasonable amount of protein, plenty of vegetables and fruit is an ideal combination. You will find your individual mix after some experimentation but as in all matters, "a little bit of what you fancy" stimulates your appetite and interest in food. We are all individuals and our needs in food are as changeable as our emotions. The food you enjoy as a 40 year-old differs markedly from your choice at twenty

Obesity and depression

Many overweight people feel self-conscious and avoid going to public places. They also may avoid taking part in activities such as travelling in buses or planes as the seats are too narrow. Being overweight and perceiving oneself as unattractive, hearing nasty remarks, feeling discriminated against in applying for jobs, can over many years eventually lead to low-esteem, anxiety and even depression.

The hidden dangers of sugars and carbohydrates

If you are depressed, you will benefit from eating a sugar-reduced diet. Studies indicate that the symptoms of hypoglycaemia, or low blood sugar, can destabilise your mood. Too much sugar can make you agitated, tired, shaky and weak. These symptoms result from a sudden drop in blood sugar, or hypoglycaemia. In attempting to restore your balance and satisfy your sugar cravings, you may be tempted to eat even more sugary food or low value carbohydrates, which worsens the situation.

Instead of sweets, cakes, biscuits, sweet buns, chips, and soft drinks, try to eat small amounts of protein and complex carbohydrates such as whole grains, cereals and lentils. This choice of diet will give you a more stable blood sugar level. Eating both carbohydrates and sugars has only a temporary effect in lifting brain serotonin levels. As serotonin in depression is low, no wonder depressed people crave them.

Protein

Proteins are an essential brain food. When proteins break down they form amino acids that help feed the brain. Protein is found in meat, milk and milk products, egg, poultry, and fish. It can also be obtained from plant or vegetable foods such as lentils, soybean and soybean products, beans and nuts.

Oils

We all know about the harmful effect of excess saturated fat, renowned for causing high cholesterol and blocked arteries. The body requires about 20 per cent of its calories in fats but not any fats. The most important and valuable fats for the brain are omega 3 fatty acids. If you do not eat a lot of oily fish, such as salmon, mackerel, herring and sardines, fish oil supplements are an alternative. Consider visiting a natural therapist or nutritionist to establish the correct amount of fish oil necessary.

Antioxidants

Foods containing antioxidants have been linked to improvement of general health. Antioxidants counteract harmful free radicals that are linked to ageing, disease and reduced mental functioning.

The most important antioxidants are found in:

Vitamin C – oranges, kiwi fruit, tomatoes, blueberries, raspberries, strawberries and cabbage.
Vitamin E – nuts, wheat germ, leafy greens, cereal, avocados
Beta carotene – an antioxidant that is found in carrots, sweet potatoes, spinach, pumpkin, peaches, broccoli, apricots and mangoes.

Food allergies

The view held by natural medicine is that food allergies can cause headaches, gastrointestinal distress, dizziness, anxiety, mood swings and may even trigger depression. However this concept is not fully accepted by the majority of medical doctors. If you believe you have food allergies, have tests to make certain. The foods most commonly subject to allergies are dairy products and gluten, but there are many others, such as strawberries, bananas, citrus fruits, peanuts and chocolate. As each person who has food allergies is sensitive to different foods have your tests performed by a specialist in this area.

EXERCISE

Your body is like a machine that houses your thoughts, feelings and emotions and it needs looking after. It needs to be kept at an optimal level of functioning. Eating well and doing some exercise will keep you in trim. The healthier your body, the more able you will be to cope with stresses and illness.

Regular exercise is a simple, natural and effective way of relieving depression symptoms. Recently there has been a great deal of interest in the positive effect of exercise on depression. Many studies have shown that even walking briskly each day can be beneficial. Aerobic exercise such as power walking, cycling or jogging, and strength training are all beneficial for depression. Not only does exercise lift energy levels but it encourages sleep and can be a pleasant social activity as well.

If you don't enjoy exercise

Some people find exercise a chore and dislike even the idea of it. They may also consider it a waste of time. If you are one of those people who never liked partaking in sport, even at school, and avoid all exercise, you have company. You are one of many who promise themselves that they will start walking or going to the gym the next day or next week and never get there.

Blocks to exercising

If you have been unable to stick to exercising in the past try to figure out what's stopping you. You may feel self-conscious or uncomfortable exercising with others watching. If so, try exercising at home. If working out with a partner helps you to keep to your goal, try to find one. Make certain that you are not trying to find excuses. Most of us do that. Never let missing one day of your routine stop you or become an excuse for not meeting your goal.

Another approach

Stop thinking that exercising means going to a gym and working out. It doesn't. Be creative and think of something active that is fun or at least enjoyable. The activity you chose may be something you have never tried before or it could be something you once liked but haven't thought about. These are some suggestions:

- Join a group and let the social side of the exercising become important such as in a bush walking club.
- Joining a team playing bowls or badminton.
- Dancing whether it is ballroom or jazz ballet may suit you.
- You might enjoy swimming in a heated pool.
- Walking is one of the best exercises of all.

- If you need a challenge try rock climbing, water or snow skiing.
- In the end its activity that is important.

Check with your doctor

Before embarking on any strenuous exercise always check with your doctor that your body is able to withstand the demands of the activity. Discuss concerns about an exercise program and how it fits into your overall treatment plan. If you feel unwell while exercising always see your doctor.

Positive physical effects of exercise

Exercise has many positive effects on your general health: improving your heart and lung function, increasing your muscle strength, your flexibility and endurance. It helps to keep your weight in check, lowers stress and promotes sound sleep. Becoming fitter can make you feel healthier, look better and lift your confidence.

If you can, exercise outdoors but consider hiring or buying an exercise bicycle or treadmill as a back-up for those cold wet days. To prevent boredom, vary your program where possible.

An exercise goal

Always set your goal according to your ability and the type of activity you enjoy. Your chosen activity ought to become part of your daily life. Decide the length of time you want to devote to exercise each day. If possible, work out at the same time every day. If you haven't exercised for some time, start slowly with five minutes of regular exercise and build up increasing by a few minutes every day or as you feel comfortable. Soon you will reach your goal.

Healing story: *Beauty Within*

A petite woman sat awkwardly on the edge of the chair. She had been referred to me for counselling by a local doctor. From her gold sandals to her styled black hair and painted lips she was immaculate. She shifted her position several times and flicked a lock of hair from her forehead.

"I've never been to someone like you before...I'm not sure why I'm here," she said.

I explained that her doctor must've thought that talking to someone like me might help her. She nodded and began to speak. "I'm not feeling myself, and I'm not used to that. I'm usually a calm and organized person," she said hesitantly. Gradually she told me about herself. She had trained as an accountant but later she worked in the family business. Since she'd stopped work she had become depressed.

"My husband, Stephen felt that I'd worked long enough and my place was in the home." She sighed and shifted her position again. "But my life is empty. We were childhood sweethearts at university. We put all our efforts into our two children and into developing our business, but now that the children are married and the business almost runs itself without us, we have nothing in common. Lately we have been like strangers in the same house. I no longer love him but we have done what's expected of us by our families, maintained the shell of the marriage and kept up appearances for the children. I guess we will stay together because our business affairs are linked."

She stared at the carpet. "I suppose it was a good idea to come here. I need to sort things out." She smoothed the creases in her skirt. "I'm not sure whether missing my work turned my thoughts back to my youth... when I was lonely and afraid. Pictures from the past haunt me...when I lie awake at night and in my dreams. Sometimes it seems as if I'm still that child obeying my parents, whispering behind my hands in communist controlled Hungary. I was nine years old when the people poured through the streets in their masses to demonstrate against the government. My father was a university lecturer with subversive leanings, who had to lie low or they would have locked him up. Many thousands of people were imprisoned and some executed after the revolution. None of us felt safe at that time."

She sighed before explaining that even after the revolution was crushed, she was terrified of the soldiers in uniforms. Whenever they walked past the house, she dashed into her bedroom and hid under the covers. A few months after the suppression of the revolution her family left Hungary. They spent a year in a refugee camp in Austria and then left for Australia, where she completed high school. She smiled for the first time as she told me that she had excelled academically and decided to go to university to study accountancy. It was there that she met Stephen.

I asked how she felt now, after having lived in Australia for so many years and been successful in both business and in her career as an accountant.

"I was confident in my accountancy practice and handled complex cases without any nervousness at all....but now my childhood memories have popped out of nowhere," she said as her tears spoiled her make up. "Whenever I see a policeman or a soldier the memories come back. It's stupid but I can't help it."

Her loss of control seemed to startle her, and she rose quickly. "Its time for me to leave. I'll phone for another appointment," she said rather stiffly, trying to regain her composure.

I saw Shari two weeks later. She appologised for talking so much in our first session."For the first time in many years I talked about myself...and I can't understand my outpouring of emotion. I'm a person who doesn't express feelings openly and I think that I said more than I intended to."

Distractedly, she folded a few pleats in her dress and her expression became worried. "I haven't been feeling well the last few days. I've hardly slept and I've felt as if something has grabbed my stomach and my chest and held me so tight that I can't breathe. It's scary but I don't want to take the tablets my doctor gave me. I don't like tablets...maybe you can recommend something else that will help."

I suggested meditation to help her to relax. "It could also give you a safe place in your mind you could go to when you are afraid," I said. After demonstrating a simple form of relaxation she promised to try it.

After a several sessions, she appeared more at ease. She had been doing her meditation and had also started writing about her feelings in a journal. She looked pleased as she revealed that she had been talking to Stephen about how she felt. She found that he had unhappy memories too and they had a lot more than she'd thought to share.

For Shari it was a slow process of talking about her past, and putting her fears aside. In her last of several sessions she smiled before speaking. "I'm not scared of police anymore. They are just ordinary men and women doing a job to secure the city."

She had become involved in voluntary work by then and her depression had left her. "Perhaps I have to be more open to experience the world around me and be prepared to take a few small risks," she said. "I'm getting there...slowly."

TWENTY-THREE
꙰

IMPROVING SLEEP

Sleep problems and depression are often associated. It is not certain whether depression causes the sleep problems or if problems sleeping occurred first. Studies show that sufferers of severe depression have marked sleep disturbances.

The two distinct phases of sleep necessary for rest:

1. *Rapid eye movement (REM) or dream sleep* – a period of sleep where the eyes move rapidly part of the time and when dreaming occurs the brain registers intense activity. In healthy people REM sleep usually occurs 90 minutes after the start of sleep.

2. *Non – Rapid eye movement (non-REM) sleep* – a period of deep restful sleep. The normal period of Non-REM is made up of four stages, with each stage lasting from approximately 5 to 15 minutes. During these phases of non-REM sleep the body rests and regenerates. Though older people often sleep less, studies show that their need for sleep doesn't lessen.
   Most people begin to sleep with a phase of non-REM sleep followed by a brief period of REM or dream sleep. In depressed people REM sleep tends to occur earlier. According to researchers into sleep in depressed people, early REM sleep results in the first cycle of non-Rem sleep, the period of greatest rest for the mind and body, being briefer than usual. The more severe the depression, the earlier REM sleep begins. In depressed people it may start after 45 minutes. Deep sleep is not recovered or made up later during the sleep cycle and less rest occurs.

Common sleep difficulties

Many depressed people complain that they lie in bed at night with their minds churning over the day's events or anticipating difficulties the next day.

You may take a long time to fall asleep and it is common to experience interrupted sleep or wake during the night, so that your total sleep time is reduced and you have little or no deep sleep. You may have trouble falling asleep again, or wake in the early hours of the morning and then feel tired for the rest of the day.

How much sleep is enough?

Everybody's needs are different. Generally five to six hours sleep is probably a minimum and below that your performance at work and driving may be affected. Most people need between seven and eight hours sleep a night to feel refreshed. Generally, people require less sleep the older they get. But it isn't the total amount of sleep that matters. Your best quality sleep occurs in the first five hours.

Sleep deprivation

If you suffer from sleep deprivation it can result in:

- Impaired memory and thought processes.

- Increased depression.

- Decreased immune system responses.

- Fatigue.

- Increased perception of pain.

Some causes of insomnia

- Alterations to the body's circadian rhythm or internal clock due to shift work or jet lag can cause daytime fatigue and difficulty falling asleep.

- Noise or an uncomfortably hot or poorly ventilated room can disturb sleep.

- Daytime naps can make you too alert for sleep later.

- Certain antidepressants can cause insomnia, so discuss this with your doctor.

- If possible, avoid using all sleeping tablets. Prolonged use of sleeping tablets may cause physical and psychological dependence. They lose their effectiveness over time and you may need an increasing amount to fall asleep. In the end you could be left with your insomnia.

If you have not been able to sleep at all for three days or more, it is advisable to see a doctor.

What to do about insomnia

- For a good night's sleep, slow yourself down before you go to bed, and do any last minute tasks in a leisurely fashion. Don't rush to bed early in the hope of a longer sleep, because you are likely to find yourself lying awake while you try to quieten down.

- Do not work on a computer or cell phone as this stimulates rather than relaxes.

- About an hour or more before bedtime, practise relaxation, read a calming book or have a warm bath with essential oils such as lavender, bergamot, chamomile or sandalwood and you will be in a calm frame of mind, ready for sleep.

- Try to develop a pattern – go to sleep and get up the same time every day during the week and on weekends, and don't lie in bed.

- Your body needs to establish a sleep rhythm. Exercise during the day is helpful, but not two to three hours before bedtime.

- Avoid alcohol, coffee and cigarettes late at night because they are stimulants and may disturb your sleep.

- Doing deep breathing during the day is a good idea, as it will help you to drop your overall stress levels.

- Deep breathing in bed is a useful aid in promoting relaxing sleep.

- Practice mindful relaxation before sleep.

- Try not to eat a large, rich meal before bed, as it will interfere with your digestion and your sleep. The best snack at bedtime is a biscuit or cracker with a warm, milky drink.

- Most important of all, if you find that you can't sleep after thirty minutes, get up, go to another room and do something boring or repetitive for a while, then go back to bed. Repeat this process during the night, if necessary.

- Keep a sleep journal.

A sleep journal

Keeping a daily sleep journal helps you to evaluate your progress and assess your sleep problems. Observing your sleep-wake pattern will reassure you that you are getting more sleep than you thought. Your sleep diary is also useful as a record to show your counsellor, doctor or psychiatrist to explain your sleep difficulties.

A TYPICAL SLEEP JOURNAL

	Causes of insomnia	Sleep Time	Number of Sleep hours	Times woke	Waking Time	How you felt all day
23 Jan	Headache.	12.30	4 hours	2	4.30	Tired, irritable.
24 Jan	Worrying.	1.15	3.5 hours	1	4.45	Couldn't concentrate, very tired.
25 Jan.	Slept in afternoon.	3.00	4 hours	0	7.00	Tired.
26 Jan	Exercised late.	12.00	5 hours 10 mins.	2	5.10	Reasonable.

Practice mindful relaxation before sleep

Mindful relaxation can help you to improve your sleep. When you are ready for sleep, notice the position of your body in the bed, how your head is placed on the pillow and the feeling of heaviness from blankets or covers. Ask yourself if your position and level of warmth or cool is comfortable. If not, move about and correct it.

Now turn your attention to your thoughts. Are you continuing to think of something that happened during that day? Or are you worried or fearful? Perhaps your thoughts are racing. If thoughts are preventing you from sleeping, merely observe them. Ask yourself if they are important enough to get out of bed and write them down to remember to work on the next day or let them go.

Now check whether you are retaining tension anywhere. Are you in pain or discomfort?

Being aware of your mind and body can help you to improve your ability to fall asleep and the quality of your sleep as well. Refer to the section on Mindfulness and follow the methods suggested for concentrating on your breathing and letting thought interferences leave you. You will also find that these exercises can allow you to sleep and even improve any physical discomfort. Repeat the exercise as often as necessary. With practice you will find the exercises easier, your ability to deal with distractions and discomfort better and sound sleep will become far less of a problem.

Healing story: *Imagination fired*

Emelia lived alone in a cottage that had once been her grandmother's. It was situated on a tract of land on the fringe of a town, nestling at the foot of the mountains. During the day she worked in the large garden, tending a wide variety of flowers and vegetables as her grandmother had done. Some produce she kept and the rest she sold at the village market. Apart from the pleasure gained in touching the delicate blooms, admiring their colours and sniffing their scents, nothing much interested her. She carried the burden of a heavy ache and whether the sun shone brightly or it rained, she seemed unaffected. She raked the ground, turned the soil and planted seedlings automatically. Her parents had been killed by a landslide when she was little, and her elderly grandmother died when she was in her late teens. She was an only child, alone and disconnected from the world. Her only interest lay in her rich fantasy life.

Emelia's daydreams of a warm and loving mother began when she started school – a mother who smiled and waved when she went off in the morning, and kissed her when she returned. A caring teacher became the focus of her fantasies. When the teacher became pregnant, Emalia would watch her round tummy growing and imagine she was inside it, warm and wanted. She missed the teacher when she left to have her baby but her daydreams about the baby's birth and even the room it slept in continued to dominate her thinking. She chose a pastel pink room with candy striped curtains, a white bassinette and a huge, cuddly teddy bear. Later, when she grew into a woman, other fantasies of being in a loving environment developed, and she filled her daily thoughts with an imaginary husband and family based on pictures she had seen in magazines.

One year, fierce rains swamped the flowers in the garden and then swirling winds uprooted all the vegetables. With nothing to sell at the market she feared she would starve during the winter. Unused to dealing with such huge practical problems, she did nothing but stare at the sodden ground and sigh. When almost all her store of food was eaten, her first reaction was to think of escaping, and she daydreamed of climbing to the highest point of the nearby hill and throwing herself into the ravine below. She had thought of that many times before. During her restless nights she dreamed of her dead body lying rotting and undiscovered in the ravine.

Hunger woke her early one morning and she ate the last bit of bread. She paced the small sitting room until the afternoon, when suddenly fired with energy, she hurried to the nearby forest. She studied the trees. Could she use a few pine branches and berries to make something beautiful, she asked herself. She stared at the trees again, gathered berries, mushrooms, other plants and left.

She woke the following day with an idea. "Perhaps I could put a winter posy together of all the lovely branches in the forest and even sell it at the market," she said to herself. It seemed like a silly idea and she pushed it away.

After returning to the forest with her basket to search for food, she sat on the soft earth, surrounded by the lovely pines, tall spruces and beeches. She sighed and stretched. Then she cut pine branches, berries and other decorative leaves and put them in her basket. There was a patch of yams growing wild and she collected those too.

The yams and mushrooms made a tasty stew and sustained her as she worked furiously putting the leaves and branches together. Her imagination was stirred and there was no room for fantasy that night. Once she had assembled the foliage, she found lace and velvet ribbons in her grandmother's old sewing basket to tie the decorative posies she'd made.

She woke hours later afraid. "A stupid idea. No one will want my posies. I won't sell any," she told herself. Nevertheless she persisted and arrived early at the market. Initially there was no interest in what she had to sell. But by mid-morning when the town's ladies came to market, they were fascinated with her unusual creations. "Aren't they lovely, so different. My posy will go nicely in my living room," she heard them say. Nearly all her posies were sold and she went straight to the store to buy food.

"What a marvellous imagination you have," the woman at the store said to her. "I'd never have thought of taking a few leaves and putting them together in that way."

Emalia walked back to the cottage, her mind charged with ideas of things she could make to sell at the market. In the months that followed, her confidence grew from making and selling her own creative products. In her spare moments she fantasised about her brief conversations with the people she met at the market. Gradually her inner ache eased and her life began to take on a new direction.

PART 6

TREATMENT FOR DEPRESSION

TWENTY-FOUR

TRADITIONAL TREATMENT FOR DEPRESSION

When to seek help

It is not a sign of weakness to admit that you or a loved one feels overwhelmed by depression. Admitting how you feel and doing something about it is the rational action to take. It is time to seek professional help if you have any of the following symptoms:

- You feel overwhelmed by despair and hopelessness. You are unusually tired over weeks or months, even though you are sleeping longer than usual.

- Your life seems out of control and you aren't coping with your personal relationships or work.

- There are changes in your appetite and sleep patterns are physical signs that you need help.

- When you can't seem to recover from a stressful event, such as an accident or a relationship break-up.

Seek help immediately if your depression has progressed to the stage of thinking about death and suicide. Don't wait another moment.

Case study

This is how Sara described her first experience of counselling:

"I couldn't sleep much the night before my appointment because I wasn't sure what to expect. I had no idea how the psychologist could help me to feel better, or if anyone could. Driving to the counsellor I thought of all the things I wanted to talk about, but when I arrived I couldn't remember any of them.

It was scary seeing a psychologist for the first time. I was worried that maybe I was really crazy, to need to see someone like that. You know, there's all that stigma about getting psychological help. I've always thought that you should solve your own problems. It's a method that's worked for me up till now...but I guess there comes a time when you can't handle things any more, not on your own. You realise that you have to face things that are bothering you.

Trust is important, so important. The minute I walked in that room I felt safe. I knew it would be OK. I needed that understanding; for someone to listen and tell me it would be all right...that the things I was thinking and feeling weren't weird. I cried a lot in the beginning, but once I'd let it all out, I felt calmer. I don't really know how it all worked, but it must have been a combination of sharing things, and learning new ways of thinking and coping. It wasn't always easy but I trusted her. I ended up doing all the work, helping myself, but she was there, guiding, suggesting, encouraging...always prepared to listen. The main thing is that I seem to be over that awful feeling, except for the odd down day. Yes, I guess I could say it was worthwhile."

The prize-winning novelist, William Styron, captures the feelings of many who are concerned about having therapy: *"I had never consulted a mental therapist for anything, and I felt awkward; also a bit defensive; my pain had become so intense that I considered it quite improbable that conversation with another mortal, even with one with professional expertise in mood disorders, could alleviate the distress."*

Different therapists who treat depression

Your general practitioner will usually recommend an appropriate health professional for you to consult. If you are severely depressed, and have a history of suicide attempts, or feel suicidal, it is almost certain that you will be referred to a psychiatrist for assessment and treatment. If yours is a less serious form of depression, your general practitioner may suggest that he or she treats and monitors your depression himself. Your doctor may choose to treat you with or without medication, and refer you to a psychologist for counselling. It is important to discuss all recommendations made about your treatment and suggested referrals with your doctor. As we are individuals, no single approach will suit everyone suffering from depression. Fortunately, though, if you don't improve using one method of attack, another is likely to help you.

There are several types of health professionals qualified to treat depression, each of whom has a different approach to the problem. These are some of the traditional practitioners you may come across.

Psychiatrists

Psychiatrists are qualified medical doctors who have chosen to specialise in the diagnosis and treatment of psychological illnesses. Their approach is medical and they have a great deal of knowledge about medications to treat the troubled mind. In the case of severe depression, they usually prescribe antidepressants alone or with other medications. Often they recommend therapy as well. They also make decisions about whether to hospitalise a patient in situations of crisis.

Psychologists

Psychologists are not medical doctors but they have degrees with psychology subjects as their major areas of study and have also completed postgraduate training. An increasing number of psychologists have doctoral degrees. They are required to be licensed members of their state's psychological council or board in order to practise. A consultation with a psychologist involves talking about your experiences, feelings, and fears. The psychologist's expertise is in listening to you, and understanding your way of interacting with the world around you and the difficulties you may have. A psychologist assesses your problem areas and works with you to develop strategies to help you cope with them. If your thoughts are negative, you will be helped to think more constructively. If you feel anxious, despairing and lost, you'll be supported. Problems such as depression, anxiety, low self-esteem, stress, panic, expressing aggression, and relationship difficulties are some of the areas that a psychologist may address with you.

Social workers, nurses and other therapists

Many people claim to be therapists or counsellors. It is unwise, however, to be treated by a person who has no specific training, so always check their qualifications. Many social workers have worked in the mental health field and provide excellent therapy; however, they should be licensed to practise by their local professional governing council.

Alternative practitioners

You may want to consult a naturopath, acupuncturist, masseur or kinesiologist in addition to any other therapy you are receiving or in combination with it. For your protection, always check any therapist's qualifications and level of experience and inform your medical doctors of other practitioners treating you.

Whether you are cared for by your doctor or you elect to be treated by one or more health professionals, the aim is the same: to help you to recover.

MEDICAL TREATMENT

Once the type of depression is diagnosed by a doctor, a suitable method of treatment can be chosen. These are the treatments that a doctor or psychiatrist might chose to treat specific types of depression:

- Antidepressants.
- Medication for bipolar depression.
- Electroconvulsive therapy (ECT).
- Transcranial magnetic stimulation (TMS).

Antidepressant medications

If your depression is severe or it is not responding to psychological therapies, your general practitioner or psychiatrist might prescribe antidepressant medication. Doctors are the only professionals who can prescribe this type of medication. It is natural to feel uncertain about taking medication so discuss any concerns you have with your doctor.

If you are taking antidepressants for the first time, you may feel uncomfortable taking tablets or that you are "giving in" and have stopped fighting your depression. Antidepressant medication, when prescribed to suit your type of depression, will in most cases lessen the severity, and length of your depression.

Types of antidepressants

- Each group has different components and targets different aspects of depression.

- Some have side effects and interactions with other medications and can be dangerous or interfere with the effect of other medications you might be taking. For this reason never use a friend's tablets or try to buy them through the internet as each one has to be specifically prescribed to suit your condition.

- If you are pregnant and taking antidepressant medication, speak to your doctor immediately. The doctor may take you off antidepressants altogether or decide to change your medication.

- The side effects of these antidepressant medications, their possible dangers and interactions with other medications are not covered in this chapter as it is a medical matter to be discussed with your doctor, and therefore beyond the scope of this self-help book. It is however useful to be aware of the wide range of medications available to treat depression.

The following is a list of some of the more popularly prescribed antidepressant medications, giving their chemical name and trade name in brackets. All medications will have the same generic names in other countries but they may have different trade names.

Selective Serotonin Reuptake Inhibitors (SSRIs)

SSRls are regarded as highly effective in treating depression. The first SSRI antidepressant to gain the public's attention was Prozac. Among the most commonly prescribed SSRls in Australia are:

- Sertraline (Zoloft)
- Citalopram (Cipramil, Citazil, Talchexal)
- Paroxetine (Aropax, Paxtine)
- Fluoxetine (Prozac, Erocarp, Lovan, Zactin, Auscarp)
- Flovoxamine (Luvox, Faverin)

Serotonin and noradrenaline reuptake inhibitors (SNRs)

- Venlafaxine (Effexor and Effexor-XR)

Reversible inhibitors of monoamine oxidase- A(RIMAs)

- Monoclobermide (Aurorix, Anima)

Noradrenaline-serotonin specific antidepressants (NASSAs)

- Mirtazapine (Avanza, Remeron)
- They are relatively new antidepressants

Tricyclics include:

- Imipramine (Tofranil)
- Clomipramine (Dothep, Prothiaden)
- Nortriptyline (Allegron)
- Amitriptyline (Endep,Tryptanol)

Monamine Oxidase Inhibitors (MOAIs)

- Pheneizine sulphate (Nardil)
- Tranylcyromine (Parnate)

These antidepressants are usually prescribed by psychiatrists

How do antidepressants work?

They are designed to increase the concentration of the neurotransmitters or chemical messengers in the brain. The most well-known of these, serotonin and norepinephrine (noradrenaline), reduce some of the imbalances in brain chemistry that are a feature of depression.

Side-effects of antidepressants

Individuals respond quite differently to antidepressant medications, so do not be alarmed if you read a list of possible side-effects. If you do have reactions, they are usually mild and disappear after a few weeks of taking the medication. Contact your doctor if you have any severe side effects.

How soon do they take effect?

Antidepressants do not have an immediate effect. However you are likely to experience some improvement within two to six weeks of beginning treatment, though sometimes it can take as long as eight weeks. It is important to take the medication in the dosage prescribed so that you can get the maximum benefit. If the antidepressant is not having the desired effect, your doctor may increase the dosage or change the type. Bear in mind that there are a wide variety of antidepressants available and each person reacts differently to a particular form of medication.

How long does one continue taking them?

If this is your first depressive episode and you are starting to recover, you may still need to stay on antidepressants for a few months, depending on your doctor or psychiatrist's assessment. Some people who have already experienced major depression, become depressed again within the next two or three years. If your doctor or psychiatrist considers you are at risk of developing recurrent depression, he may suggest that you stay on medication for long periods or indefinitely. It is best to discuss the likelihood of a relapse, the severity of the attack, its duration and issues such as a family history of depression with your doctor. All play an important part in deciding whether it is necessary for you to stay on medication or not.

Medication together with counselling

Medication and counselling complement each other in treating depression. Counselling aims to change negative thought patterns, build self-esteem and helps you to deal with issues that hamper your ability to cope. It reinforces the gains made by the medication, enabling you to make positive changes in your life. If you are severely depressed, a total approach, addressing both emotional and physical aspects, is a sensible and positive route to recovery.

Case study

Mary is depressed and has been seeing a psychologist for about a year. Although she has gained a great deal from counselling, she continues to feel despairing and hopeless. It is obvious that counselling alone is unable to shift her mood. She rarely takes an aspirin for a headache and has been against taking antidepressant medication from the start, even though her doctor recommended it. When her counsellor suggests that an antidepressant may help to lift her mood, she decides to speak to her doctor about it again. After a thorough evaluation, he prescribes the medication.

Two weeks after taking the medication Mary complains, "I haven't noticed anything positive yet. I have a dry mouth and I'm constipated. It's unpleasant. Maybe I shouldn't have taken the tablets. Dr Liebowitz says that these are mild side-effects from the tablets that will go in a few weeks. I certainly hope so."

Three weeks later, she says, "I can feel something good is happening to me, but I can't put my finger on it. I think I'm calmer, more stable, but

I'm not really happy. That heavy feeling has gone and at least I've stopped crying...that really embarrassed me. Yeah, my mind is a bit clearer and I can concentrate enough to read the newspaper for the first time in ages. I don't have the energy to do much yet but I hope that I'll have some soon."

She gives me a half smile. "I'm pleased I took the antidepressants. You know, it's strange, that all the things we talk about in our sessions seem to make more sense now."

"What about the side-effects?" I ask.

"Oh, they're not bothering me much at all now."

Electroconvulsive therapy (ECT)

Electroconvulsive therapy plays a valuable role in the treatment of people who are severely or suicidally depressed. It is a life-saving option for a suicidal person when a three to six-week wait for antidepressants to take effect may be too long or too risky. ECT may also be recommended for severely depressed people who cannot take antidepressant medications due to their side-effects or for those who do not improve with other forms of therapy. For pregnant women with major depression, electroconvulsive therapy is regarded as preferable to medication, which could harm the foetus.

As a result of its reputation of harsh and inappropriate use in the 1940s and 1950s, electroconvulsive therapy has been regarded with fear and suspicion, but with the modern techniques and equipment used today it is now a safer, pain-free and effective treatment that can bring about improvements in depression in a few weeks.

What happens during ECT?

First you are given a thorough medical examination. The procedure is explained and your consent is obtained. ECT is usually administered in a hospital or out-patient clinic. An anaesthetic and muscle relaxing drug is administered before a low voltage electrical current is passed through electrodes that are placed on your head. This electrical stimulation creates brain wave changes which affect the neurotransmitters serotonin and norepinephrine (noradrenaline) and other chemicals involved in depression. The resulting chemical reactions are responsible for changes in your mood.

After the treatment you may be briefly confused and forgetful or uncertain of events immediately before it took place. Within two or three weeks your memory should return to normal. Longer-term memory deficits are rarely reported.

If necessary electroconvulsive therapy can be administered three times a week for up to twelve treatments.

Transcranial Magnetic Stimulation

Tanscranial magnetic stimulation (TMS) is a new form of treatment for depression, utilizing an electromagnet placed on the scalp that generates magnetic field pulses, roughly the strength of an MRI scan. The magnetic pulses pass through the skin and skull, stimulating the underlying cerebral cortex. There are no side effects from the treatment. It is a 40-minute outpatient procedure that is prescribed by a psychiatrist. The treatment is typically administered daily for 4 – 6 weeks.

MEDICAL TREATMENT FOR BIPOLAR DISORDER (MANIC DEPRESSION)

Treatment of bipolar disorder depends on the seriousness of the symptoms and the duration of the illness. Treatment is usually by a psychiatrist and finding the appropriate medication is the key to treating this disorder.

Psychotherapy helps you to develop strategies for use during periods of elation, so that unwanted behaviour that could later cause you to feel; regret and shame is avoided. Equally, during a depressed phase you can master techniques that will keep you more active and motivated and help to smooth out the roller coaster experience of living with a bipolar disorder.

Medication

Lithium carbonate

Lithium carbonate is a mood stabiliser used to treat both manic and depressed episodes, and as a maintenance therapy between episodes to prevent both highs and lows reoccurring. The exact way in which lithium stabilises the brain is unknown, but its effectiveness is well established, with a success rate of about 70 per cent of patients. Your treating psychiatrist may consider it necessary to add other medications to lithium to dampen your mania or antidepressants to lift your mood during the depressive phase. If side-effects do occur they are most likely to develop during the early stages of taking the medication.

Anticonvulsants

Anticonvulsants, originally developed for the treatment of epilepsy, are frequently used in the treatment of bipolar disorder as mood stabilizers. They have been shown to relieve the symptoms of mania and reduce mood swings. These are some of the prescribed anticonvulsant medications:

- Divalproex or Valproate (Depakote, Depakene).
- Carbamazepine (Tegretol)
- Lamotrigine (Lamictal)
- Topiramate (Topamax)

Mood stabilizers

The following newer medications are frequently used now for the treatment of bipolar disorder:

- Lamictal (Lamotrigine)
- Seroquel (Quetiapine)
- Zyprexa (Olanzapine)

- Symbyax (a tablet that combines Olanzapine with the antidepressant Fluoxetine)

It is natural to feel that you are not making progress at times and to feel anxious about a possible relapse. Review your treatment and progress positively and always communicate openly with your doctor. Write down all the difficulties that you are having and take the list with you when you visit your doctor, so that all your concerns receive attention. If your antidepressant is not having the required effect or you are experiencing unpleasant reactions, don't be afraid to discuss it. Your doctor may decide to change it for another type or add another medication.

If you haven't seen a counsellor yet, consider doing so. You can ask for a referral from your doctor or phone for an appointment. Talking to someone who understands your problem, who can help you to develop some new coping techniques, may make all the difference.

TWENTY-FIVE

⁂

PSYCHOLOGICAL THERAPIES FOR DEPRESSION

How to choose a counsellor

The first place to start your search for a counsellor is through your general practitioner, who is likely to have a list of counsellors with a good record of success with his patients. You can also find a competent counsellor through personal recommendation, from the Psychological Society in your state or in the Yellow Pages. When you have several names of possible counsellors, phone each one to briefly discuss your problem and evaluate their responses. This discussion is likely to help you decide which of the counsellors suits you best. Of course, experience and credentials are essential in a counsellor, but the most important consideration of all is whether you feel comfortable talking to him and believe that he can help you.

Different therapists will use the particular approach they find most suitable to treat your depression. These are the most popular therapies:

Cognitive behavioural therapy (CBT)

Cognitive behavioural therapy is a brief therapy, widely and successfully used to treat depression. It is a practical and problem-solving therapy, based on the here and now, and it teaches you that depression is the result of unquestioned unproductive thoughts and attitudes. CBT will increase your awareness of your destructive thoughts that are linked to your depression, and help you to replace them with rational, constructive ones. It will assist you to recover a gradual interest in pleasurable activities, make important lifestyle changes and teach you ways of developing your self-esteem and assertiveness. Most importantly it will make you aware of early warning signs of a recurrence of your depression and provide you with a plan of how to prevent it taking hold once more.

Mindfulness-based Cognitive Therapy (MBCT)

This form of therapy is a mixture of two different therapeutic approaches – cognitive behavioural therapy (CBT) and mindfulness – based cognitive therapy (MBCT). MBCT is a fairly recent add-on approach to CBT that has gained popularity.

Mindfulness therapy developed mainly from Buddhist meditative practice. It allows you to gain control over the processes of thinking in a neutral and detached way. It does this through learning to be aware of thoughts and physical sensations in the moment and creates awareness, acceptance and acknowledgement of past and present events or experiences without reacting to them, judging or analysing them.

Psychoanalysis

Psychoanalysis is an older form of therapy that focuses on resolving deep-seated conflicts from the past. As it may take as long as a few years for a person to benefit from it, it is not considered a practical therapy for an acutely depressed person who is overcome with feelings of hopelessness, is unable to sleep, eat or muster the energy to cope with life.

However psychoanalysis may be helpful if you are mildly depressed or dissatisfied with life and seeking answers to your present malaise in your past.

Interpersonal therapy

This form of therapy emphasises problems with close relationships. It deals with the way you handle grief and loss; changes in roles, namely becoming a parent, starting a new job and handling unresolved disputes. It is a therapy that helps you to improve your communication skills.

New forms of therapy

Online Therapy

Therapy is now available online so that you can interact with a therapist on your iPhone or on your computer. There are also online forms of therapy available that follow a self-help approach giving you a step by step guide of CBT. These methods are an excellent start but cannot replace face-to-face counselling.

Thermal camera face analysis

UC Associate Professor Roland Goecke has been working with the Black Dog institute in Sydney, Australia to develop a computer program that uses voice and facial recognition to diagnose depression. Sufferers of depression may soon be monitoring the severity of their condition using smartphones and digital tablets incorporating voice and facial recognition technology. The aim is to use the technology to help doctors determine an appropriate treatment program for patients. This approach may be useful in outlying areas where there is little help for sufferers of depression.

TWENTY-SIX

NATURAL MEDICINES TO TREAT DEPRESSION

Depression is not a condition with one cause or treatment. Mood and mental performance can to an extent be affected by imbalances and deficiencies in nutrition. Many people turn to natural medicine for the treatment of *mild depression*.

Natural medicine versus traditional medicine

Both approaches are of value and have their place in the treatment of depression. The choice of treatment is dependent on the severity of your condition. Less debilitating conditions, such as mild depression and some forms of reactive depression might be treated successfully with counselling and herbal medicines. However if you suffer from major depression, or bipolar depression, or other debilitating forms of depression such as postnatal depression or substance-induced depression, you are seriously ill and your doctors are likely to consider prescribing medications to bring you relief.

If you are able to manage your life, work and socialise, and your depression is mild, you may wish to consult a qualified natural practitioner about using natural medicines alone, or together with counselling. It is essential that you inform your alternative practitioner and counsellor, if you are seeing one, of all the medications you are taking (natural and prescribed), as well as the background to your depression, your symptoms and family history. Also make a point of informing your medical practitioner that you are seeking alternative treatment and tell him about any tablets you may be taking. There need be no conflict between therapeutic approaches.

The required dosages, combinations of medicines and the interactions of natural medicines with any conventional medicines or antidepressants need to be understood by qualified and experienced practitioners. Never put yourself in the hands of a natural therapist without the necessary knowledge, understanding and qualifications.

> Self-medicating is dangerous as interactions with some traditional medications can occur.

Plant based natural medicines

Throughout history and as far back as early Christian times, herbs were used for alleviating physical and emotional conditions. Today many people with uncomplicated complaints are returning to these milder treatments due to their fewer known side-effects than conventional drugs. Research in the field of natural therapies is increasing and they are becoming more accepted as genuine options, often on the fringe of mainstream medicine. The following natural medicines are often used to relieve depression:

St John's Wort (Hypericum perforatum)

St John's Wort is regarded by natural therapists as a herbal treatment for mild depression. The herb is widely used in Europe and Germany in particular, where research has been undertaken to prove its effectiveness. It is also frequently used for alleviating mild depression in Australia and the USA. The herb grows on a small bush with yellow flowers and in Germany it blossoms towards the end of June, close to St John's Day, hence its name. In ancient times the juice extracted from the plant was mainly used to heal wounds.

St John's Wort is thought to act in a similar way to some antidepressant drugs. Never take it at the same time as other medications, especially prescribed antidepressants. Always consult your doctor before taking it, as dangerous interactions with some traditional medications can occur. Though it has far fewer side-effects than some prescribed antidepressant medications, gastric upsets, allergic reactions, skin reddening, dizziness and confusion have been reported. As in the case of antidepressants, St John's Wort takes several weeks for its effect to be felt.

Some of the other herbal medicines used to treat mild depression are:

Gingko biloba, ginseng, kava, gotu, kola, borage and melissa officinalis.

As with any medications, do not take more than the recommended dose as toxic reactions may result if taken in excess.

Vitamins and minerals

Vitamins and minerals alone will not cure your depression but if you are deficient in them they will support your body and nervous system. Seek advice from a qualified herbalist or naturopath about the best way to incorporate vitamin therapy in the management of your condition, but do not self-medicate as excessive dosages of some vitamins can be dangerous.

Dr Sandra Cabot who is well-known in the field of holistic medicine recommends the following supplements for people who are depressed:

Vitamin B

All the B group vitamins with their co-factors of choline, inositol and biotin (found in most Vitamin B tablets) are essential to brain function. Without them the brain is unable to manufacture the neurotransmitters of dopamine and serotonin. Deficiencies of this vitamin can lead to depressive symptoms.

Magnesium

Magnesium is said to ease the symptoms of muscle cramps and twitches and help to relax the body. According to Dr Cabot, Magnesium with Vitamin B6 is necessary to convert the amino acid tryptophan into necessary serotonin.

Amino acids

Amino acids are sometimes used to boost levels of particular neurotransmitters or to treat anxiety and depression. Studies have shown that amino acids such as DL-phenylalanine, LTyrosine and Tryptophan are precursors of chemical neurotransmitters and can act similarly to antidepressants.

SAMe is a synthetic form of a compound formed naturally in the body. There have been a number of studies on the use of SAMe for depression. It has been hypothesized that SAMe increases the availability of neurotransmitter serotonin and dopamine but research is still in its early days.

Amino acids can have side-effects if used together with antidepressants so only take them under medical supervision.

Omega-3 fatty acids

Several individual studies link a low intake of Omega-3 fatty acids to all forms of depression. These fatty acids are found in highest concentrations in cold water fish, namely salmon, tuna, trout and mackerel. For those intolerant to fish oil, flaxseed oil contains Omega-3 fatty acids and is available in capsule or liquid form.

Homeopathic medicines

In 1810, a German physician, Samuel Hahnermann, developed the medical discipline he called homeopathy. Using minerals, natural plants and herbs, he found that by diluting them over thirty times and shaking them vigorously, they were filled with energy between dilutions. He preserved his mixtures in alcohol and used them to heal his patients. There are over 1200 homeopathic medicines with directions for their use by a practitioner.

Homeopathy is a complex system of therapy aimed at stimulating the body's ability to recover from an illness rather than treating the symptoms. There are a wide range of homeopathic medicines available for the treatment of depression. In skilled hands positive results have been recorded. Of course, as always with natural medicines, your medical doctor should be consulted, and if you are seeing a homeopath he should also be told of any prescription drugs you may be taking.

Bach flowers made from English wild flowers, the homeopathic remedies discovered in England by Dr Edward Bach in the 1920s, are believed to balance emotional conditions. The following remedies are used for various types of depression:

- *Agrimony* – for those who hide their troubles from others and seek solace from their misery through drugs and alcohol.

- *Gorse* – for feelings of hopelessness and futility.

- *Mustard* – for feelings of gloom and sadness.

- *Star of Bethlehem* – for grief, trauma or loss.

- *Elm* – for those overwhelmed and burdened by responsibility.

- *Sweet Chestnut* – for those in unbearable despair, who feel that they have reached the limit of their endurance.

- *Pine* – for those weighted down by guilt and unsatisfied by their efforts.

- *Larch* – for those who anticipate failure.

- *Rescue Remedy* – for the calming and stabilising of emotions in a crisis.

Chinese medicine

Chinese medicine views depression as an imbalance between mind and body. Therapies such as acupuncture and Chinese herbs are often effective in treating mild forms of depression and other emotional issues. Though Chinese practitioners see their treatments as a total alternative to psychiatric drugs, if your depression is very severe, it would be advisable to discuss your condition with a Western trained doctor as well as your Chinese practitioner. A good doctor of any modality welcomes other options.

Ayurvedic medicine

Ayurveda is India's traditional medicine which evolved approximately 5,000 years ago and is said to be one of the oldest and most complete medical systems. Its main aim is to prevent disease and foster health. Ayurvedic medicine treats depression with diet, herbs, massage, cleansing, purification measures and spiritual rituals.

Other therapies

There are several additional therapeutic options available to relieve the symptoms of depression. While counselling and medications are essential for helping severely depressed people, a group of other therapies can be used in conjunction with them to express feelings and balance emotions through the senses and active involvement.

Animal-assisted therapy (or pet therapy)

Animal-assisted therapy is a general term for therapeutic activities involving animals. Studies have shown that regular interaction with dogs and horses has positive benefits. Depressed people may benefit from interaction with dogs or horses, in particular. The animals give unconditional love and affection and ask for nothing in return. They are very intuitive and know just what type of interaction an individual requires. There are many reports of people who communicate little, talking to a dog or horse, or physically challenged people who reach out an arm to stroke a loved animal.

Some of the advantages of animal assisted therapy are the following:

- Decreased feelings of isolation and loneliness.
- Improved physical health due to exercise with the pet.
- Usually involves the use of fewer calming medications.
- Encourages involvement and social interaction.
- Helps to develop a sense of responsibility in caring for an animal, for example grooming and feeding.

- Encourages emotions in what can be a numbed and wooden depressed person.

- Encourages cognitive functions such as memory, emotions and speech.

- Provides comfort and brings joy and happiness.

Music Therapy

Music therapy has produced positive results for certain distressed individuals though at present there is insufficient research to back up the results claimed. It is suggested that depending on the type and intensity of the sounds, music may stimulate positive changes in brain chemistry. Music has been used to calm and delight over the centuries and it may also assist depressed individuals in conjunction with other forms of therapy undertaken.

Art Therapy

For many depressed people a lump of clay or a blank canvass can be an opportunity to express feelings that words cannot speak. Creating art allows you to feel again. Once you can view an externalised emotion it is easier to accept it as part of yourself. It may give you the opportunity to express what you cannot say. This may provide understanding, even relief.

PART 7

DEPRESSION IN SPECIAL GROUPS – CHILDREN, TEENAGERS, THE AGED, A LOVED ONE

TWENTY-SEVEN

DEPRESSION IN CHILDREN

It may not be obvious that your child is depressed, as children usually don't exhibit their sadness in the same way as adults do and are often unable to explain how they feel. However, childhood depression can occur in schoolchildren and even in toddlers and be as intense and disabling as depression in adults.

Case study

Jean Lower aged eleven, lived with both her parents and her seven year old brother, Roy. Most of the time the two children who were close in age, played together with little incident but in past months they had begun to squabble.

Jean's teachers found that though she was usually a bright, active child in class, recently she seemed withdrawn. One day after a lesson, Jean had a heated argument with a classmate, Brendon about the use of the computer they shared. She pushed him out of the way roughly and insisted on using it first. Brendon responded by pushing her back. As a result of the row, Jean sobbed and trembled and had to lie down in the sick room. The principal was so concerned that she phoned Mrs Lower to ask her to collect her daughter.

Mrs Lower had been worried about Jean lately as she was refusing to eat most of her meal, had wet her bed on a few occasions and tended to sit alone in her room. When Jean continued crying through the night her mother took her to the doctor.

The doctor talked to Jean on her own first. With her head down and speaking softly, Jean said, "Jeannie is not happy." When the doctor tried to find out what was bothering her, she shook her head, looked away and then burst into tears.

After talking to Mr and Mrs Lower, the doctor insisted on Jean seeing a child psychiatrist. Though the Lowers were shocked at first, an appointment was made for Jean at the local Children's Hospital. Mr and Mrs Lower left the doctor's upset but relieved that their daughter would soon receive the help she needed.

After a few sessions with the psychiatrist, Jean's feelings of being unloved and therefore unlovable surfaced. She was certain that her parents loved her brother Roy far more than her. She said her parents gave Roy far more love and even bigger and more expensive birthday and Christmas presents. Mr and Mrs Lower were shocked when they heard this. They thought they loved their children equally but soon realised that they needed to be more demonstrative towards Jean and that they ought to tell her how much she was loved. Mr Lower admitted that he had been spending more time with Roy as they both enjoyed sport.

A few months later the atmosphere in the Lower home was calmer and more loving. Jean and Roy played together once more. At school, Jean was active and friendly, enjoying her classes again.

Common signs of depression among children in the years up to puberty can include:

- A prolonged sad mood.
- A loss of interest in normal activities such as playing and games.
- Withdrawal both at home and school.
- Uncharacteristic behaviour such as stealing or bullying.
- Tiredness, particularly in the afternoon.
- Sleep disturbance.

- Bed wetting.

- Changes in appetite – either decreased or increased.

- Vocal outbursts and anger.

- Crying.

- Poor concentration.

Most children do not display all of these symptoms. In fact, most will have different symptoms at different times and in different settings. Some children continue to function reasonably well but mostly there is a noticeable change in involvement in school and other activities as well as a drop in academic performance.

Causes of depression in children

Genetic predisposition and environmental stresses provide a backdrop against which depression in children may develop. So if you, your partner, or a close relative suffer from depression, your child may follow the same path. Children can also develop depression following a trauma, for example the separation or divorce of parents, or death of a close relative. Many depressed children may be responding to rejection, criticism or discouragement from parents who try their best, but are unable to express their love. Difficulties coping with school and bullying may make a negative life-long impact on a child.

How to help your depressed child

- *Give your child as much support as possible,* so that he knows that you are there for him at all times and that your love for him is unconditional. Encourage him to talk about whatever is troubling him. Listening rather than giving advice or lecturing is one of the best ways of proving your love and support. A positive approach with more praise than criticism will go a long way in building up your child's self-esteem and easing his depression.

- *Learn as much as possible about depression* as the more you know about it, the better you will be equipped for caring for your child and have a better idea how to help. You will also be able to share your knowledge and understanding with your partner, family members and close friends.

- *Never feel ashamed* or blame yourself or your partner for your child's depression. Shame and self-blame often causes parents with a depressed child to deny their child's illness to extended family members and friends. Self-blame can result in tension at home and worsen your child's depression.

- *Ask for the help* you need and seek support from others where possible, so that you can take a break from being alone with your depressed child. Ask for advice from professionals such as your doctor or a welfare worker when you need it.

- *Try not to become negative and anxious* about your child's condition. Read some of the exercises in the book or the healing stories to help you. Talk openly to your partner and those who care about you or seek counselling or support if necessary. It is difficult, but in order to help your child you need to be as balanced as possible and not pass on worries and fears.

- *Teach your child basic coping skills* that enable him to deal with people, find solutions to problems and cope with difficulties that cross his path. This will equip him to handle his teenage and adult years. The best way of teaching these skills is by example, by demonstrating your own self-control and ability to handle people, problems and day to day issues.

Bullying

Bullying can be physical or verbal with its repetitive nature being the most dangerous. A child can become fearful and live in constant fear of an attack.

While there are many reasons why bullies may target a child, the main reasons are usually physical appearance or social standing within a peer group. Bullies tend to pick on children who appear different to most of the others. Targeting of a child may also be due to race and religion. It may simply be that the child is new to the school or neighbourhood and has not as yet made friends.

How to deal with school bullies

There is no single solution to bullying. It may take your child some experimenting with a variety of different responses to find the strategy that works best. If your child is old enough to try to respond to the bully, in some of the following ways:

- Don't react in any way. The bully is trying to show how much he is controlling your child's emotions, so ignore him and walk away.

- Your child's safety is of prime importance. If the bullying becomes threatening or increases and he fears being hurt, advise him to look for a way of escaping or going to one of the teachers for safety.

- Bullies can become increasingly aggressive and threatening, and should be reported to the principal and class teacher. Once teachers are aware of the situation they can be supportive and more protective towards your child until the bullying stops. Please read the chapter on cyber bullying

Childhood Suicide

Although relatively rare in children under 12, young children do attempt suicide and may do so impulsively when they are upset or angry. If your child is expressing suicidal thoughts seek help immediately.

Healing story: *Mr Woody*

The sun oozed through early clouds, blossoms were on show and every green living thing in the garden seemed to be sprouting. Ann sat on the grass and wiped away her tears. Thank goodness the summer holidays had started and she didn't have to go to school and face the nasty bullies. If they weren't pulling her plait they were making horrid remarks about her being small.

Staring vacantly at the sky she saw it – a blob circling and then like a dive bomber making its landing a few metres from her. A duck. She and the duck stared at each other. She held her ground uncertainly but it didn't squawk or show signs of attack. All she heard was a steady *pluck, pluck*. It waddled, turning itself around several times so that she could appreciate its features – whitish mottled with brown, a dark head and beak with masked eyes and bright teal stripes on its side. What a beauty! She knew it was a drake as males were always the better looking birds.

She dashed into the kitchen for bread. Her mother always left stale bread for the birds in a plastic bag. She moistened the bread, placed it on the grass and waited. Meanwhile the duck had discovered the rock pool at the top of the garden and was luxuriating in it. Only after he had shaken himself dry, preened and scanned the garden, did he nibble at the food. The raven who made his look-out in a tree hollow, surveyed the duck's movements, while the magpies gave him right of way and kept out of sight. The duck ruffled its feathers, waddled onto a grassy strip and took off.

He flew in each day of the school holidays. She looked forward to his visits and gave him the name, Mr Woody. After eating his ration of bread, he would paddle in the pool and wander around near where she played. Though her mother nagged her to ask friends around, she felt much safer on her own.

The duck was almost tame and on some days he followed her inside the house, while on others he ignored her.

"You're a strange one Mr Woody, you do exactly as you please!" She laughed as she threw the duck a piece of soft bread.

A week before school began the duck's visits stopped. Ann scoured the skies but no blob. She wondered about the duck's arrival the day holidays began and its disappearance shortly before she was due to go back to school. She knew her inner voice well. It warned her about people who were mean or criticised for doing the wrong thing. This time her inner voice told her that there was something to learn from Mr Woody's visit. "Spread your wings," the voice niggled. "And don't worry about the others."

When Ann returned to school, she walked past the bullies with her head held high, imagining she was ruffling her feathers and ignored them. She didn't even look back to see how they reacted. The bullies didn't approach her again and Ann forgot about them. Mr Woody flew in again the following year during her summer holidays. As before, a pile of soft, moist bread was there for him.

TWENTY-EIGHT

TEENAGE DEPRESSION

Teenagers dealing with hormonal changes and the complexity of our world often feel at a loss, misunderstood and confused. Though teenage years are a time to test out wings and rebel against rules, parents witnessing these changes for the first time, might feel frustrated about their teenager's lack of response to discipline and family values. Raising a teenager is an enormous challenge and it is understandable for parents to feel concerned or even afraid and helpless about their teenager's choices and actions.

Symptoms of teenage depression

The detection of depression in adolescents can be more difficult than in children. The common turmoil of adolescence may make them moody and at times withdrawn, especially as the young person is forging new roles within the family and often struggling with independence, academic or career decisions. A teenager who is depressed may not show obvious signs of depression and instead begin to behave uncharacteristically in the following ways:

- Becoming socially withdrawn.
- Cutting school.
- Failing academic performance.
- Engaging in risk-taking behaviours (e.g. reckless driving, inappropriate sexual involvements).
- Avoiding favourite activities and friends.

- Engaging in drug and alcohol abuse.

- Leaving home suddenly.

- Paying less attention to hygiene or appearance.

- Self-harm.

- Alcohol and drug abuse.

- Talking of dying or suicide.

Teenage depression versus adult depression

Teenage depression can differ from adult depression in some of these ways:

Moodiness, angry, irritable and hostile behaviour rather than sadness or unhappiness, is common.

Over sensitivity to comments and criticism is common in depressed teenagers. Their feelings of low self-esteem, worthlessness and fears of rejection make them more vulnerable and sensitive.

Moving away from family members may occur if teenagers are depressed. While not isolating themselves completely from their peer group, they may make new friends and seek out different activities.

Physical aches and pains, headaches and nausea are often present in teenagers with depression. These should always be assessed by a doctor.

How to help your depressed teenager

- *Share your concerns in a supportive way:* In a loving and non-judgmental way, try to share your concerns with your teenager. Let him know what specific signs of depression you may have noticed and tell him why they worry you. Always encourage your child to share what he is experiencing. Your teenager may be reluctant to talk to you about his depression or be ashamed or worried that you won't understand. He might deny his feelings and claim that all is well, as he may not believe that what he is going through is the result of depression.

- *Try not to lecture:* Make certain that your teenager feels that you care and that you are there for him, whatever mood he is in. Try not to question him or give lectures or he will ignore what you say. Listen instead. Do not use comparisons to other teenagers to clarify your viewpoint or offer advice.

- *Validate feelings*: Do not try to convince your teenager that his feelings are irrational or silly. Always acknowledge his pain and take his feelings seriously.

- *Seek help:* Depression is very damaging when left untreated, so do not wait and hope that the symptoms will go away. If you see depression's warning signs, ask your doctor for a referral to a psychologist or psychiatrist who specialises in treating children and teenagers or go to your city's children's hospital. Treating teenagers with medication, if necessary, needs the experience and knowledge of a professional with specific training in adolescent medicine.

- *Be flexible*: Be aware of your teenager's opinion of the therapist chosen for treatment. It is essential that your teenager connects with the person treating him. Your choice of an accredited professional may not appeal to him. If necessary ask your doctor for further referrals until a relationship with the treating professional can be established.

Do not rely on medication entirely as a treatment unless your teenager is very depressed. In mild cases of depression a talk therapy with a qualified counsellor ought to be considered. If you are struggling to make decisions about the treatment of your teenager, having a general practitioner to turn to for support and guidance is always helpful.

DEPRESSION IN TEENAGERS CAN TURN DANGEROUS

Self-harm

Adolescent depression can manifest itself in several forms of self-harm. This is a way of dealing with hurtful emotions and is often an attempt at being in control. It may seem strange but self-harm may be a way of expressing and alleviating feelings of anger, self-loathing, emptiness, guilt and low self-esteem. Many teenagers say that experiencing the pain is better than feeling nothing or numbness. After the injury there is short-lived relief. Most self-harm occurs in secret and without any attempt to seek attention. The sense of guilt and shame makes it very difficult to ask for help. Even if the wounds inflicted are not serious, your child's suffering may be intense.

The most common forms self-harm can take:

- Cutting the skin.
- Scratching the skin.
- Pricking the skin with sharp objects.
- Burning the skin.
- Picking at wounds.
- Swallowing noxious or poisonous substances.
- Hitting or knocking the body with hard objects.
- Reckless harmful behaviour including driving recklessly, unsafe sex and substance abuse.

Substance induced teenage depression

Often parents are at a loss as to why their teenager is drinking heavily or taking drugs. While you might think your child is rebelling or merely trying to fit in with his friends, there may be other reasons for his drinking or taking drugs. Depression or anxiety and an inability to cope with life might be the underlying cause.

A wide range of substances, including prescription drugs, nicotine alcohol, marijuana and illicit drugs, can create or worsen depression. Constant or continual use of substances such as alcohol, benzodiazepines, cocaine, heroin and other narcotics can initiate or worsen an existing depressed mood. Unfortunately the degree of profitability from all these substances insures that they will be available on the "black market".

Alcohol and teenage depression

Alcohol is an easy means of self-medication. It is often available in a liquor cabinet in a teenager's home. Though it is not legal for a teenager to buy alcohol, a store owner may turn a blind eye or willing friends may provide it.

Alcohol withdrawal in teenagers

Once drinking ceases, a period of withdrawal will follow with intense craving for the substance and unpleasant reactions such as tremors, rapid heart rate, agitation and hallucinations. Due to these symptoms, it is recommended that your teenager undergoes supervised withdrawal, possibly in a hospital or a detoxification centre, where trained staff are on call to assist in recovery. Attending daily sobriety groups with other teenagers and having a support buddy is an important part of the therapy. In the long term, recovery will depend to a large extent on awareness of the stresses that act as triggers for drinking. Your teenager will also need to learn how to avoid situations and people that may encourage him to drink again.

Drugs and teenage depression

For many teenagers, illicit substance use and abuse is common during their teenage years. Fortunately most adolescents who experiment with drugs do not continue on to abuse in adulthood. However, if regular drug taking begins at an early age addiction can take hold.

Each individual's vulnerability to addiction differs according to their genetic history, anxiety and depression, family relationships and group of friends. A family history of addiction and abuse, traumatic experiences and feeling of being unloved adds to any teenager's vulnerability.

Case study

Grant rubbed his bloodshot eyes and looked at me sheepishly. "I've gone and done it again, haven't I. You'd have thought I'd learn from my mistakes, but it doesn't seem that I'll ever get it," He tapped the floor with his toe. "The day before yesterday I felt so bad...like there was a huge dark hole inside me...so I did what I usually do...started on the beer. I don't know how many I had and I can't remember what happened after that. I woke at about 12.00 with this pounding head and sick feeling. Worst of all I felt...like shit." He tapped the floor again. "See, I drink to get rid of the downer but after drinking it hits me twice as hard. Sure, I kid myself that I'll stop drinking. But deep down I know I won't." He looked up at me with a frightened expression. "What scares me is if I do stop, I'll turn to drugs."

Signs and symptoms of substance abuse in teenagers

The most common signs of substance abuse in teenagers are:

- Changes in behaviour and appearance.
- Drugs becoming a preoccupation and then crowding out previously important activities.
- A drop in school attendance and academic performance.
- Loss of former energy and motivation.
- Finding a new set of friends.
- Lack of interest in appearance and personal hygiene.
- Spending more time alone in the bedroom and playing sad music or writing poetry.

- Attitudes to family members changing and becoming distant or even hostile.

- Forgetfulness, lack of coordination and inability to concentrate.

- Poor sleeping habits.

How to prevent your teenager from turning to substance abuse

The temptations of drugs are almost everywhere. The closer you family unit and the more involved you are with your teenager and the more interested in his activities, the less likely he will turn to alcohol or drugs. These are some suggestions:

- Be supportive by being there to help your teenager with any problems including difficulties at school. If he is in trouble, hopefully he will turn to you rather than to drug taking friends.

- The more open you are about subjects like drug abuse, religion and sex, the more openly he will be prepared to talk to you. Provide a good example by not drinking excessively yourself or using illegal drugs.

- Be as aware as possible of your teenager's after school plans and activities and set a time for him to be home at night. Meeting as many of his friends and their parents as possible will make it easier to be aware and interested in what he does without interfering or being too controlling.

- Though many teenagers are reluctant to spend time with their parents and siblings, encourage them to eat with the family at night and try to find time for open discussion.

Healing story: *Making choices*

At sunset, a grey-haired fisherman gathered his nets to draw in his catch. It was taxing work and after securing his fish, he walked along the water's edge. He noticed a young man sitting alone on the sand.

The next morning the man was still there. He held his head in his hands and wiped away tears. The fisherman had suffered in the past and knew the pain of despair. Wishing to offer a kind word, he walked towards the young man and sat down on the sand beside him. After some time they began to talk. Slowly and at times haltingly, searching for words that would help, the fisherman talked of the struggles and anguish of his youth. "When I was young, I had hurtful memories. I called them old bones," he said, smiling wryly. "They made noises inside me, knocking and banging to remind me they were there, never, ever letting me be free, always sharp and getting in the way...a nasty feeling."

The young man nodded.

"Maybe you've got them too... making you miserable."

The young man nodded again.

The fisherman paused again searching for the right words. "I bet you'd be happy to get rid of them."

"Sure would," the young man said, as the sand drifted through his fingers. 'But how...by magic?"

"Meet me here Sunday morning and I'll help you."

The young man stared at the fisherman and shrugged.

"I'll have my boat...we'll take it out...then you'll see," the fisherman replied with a wave.

The young man stared at the golden ball slipping over the horizon and shrugged. He didn't feel very optimistic about the fisherman's solution to his suffering, but out of curiosity he decided to meet with him.

The following Sunday, the fisherman was waiting at the boat. When they set out the sky was an endless blue and the water calm. When no land could be seen, the fisherman cut the motor. The young man looked at him quizzically, wondering what would happen.

"Sit on the edge of the boat and hold on," the fisherman said. "Close your eyes, take deep breaths of the fresh sea air and think of all those hurts lurking inside of you." He waved his arms to make his point. "All those old bones rattling inside you, taking up so much space and disturbing your life....time to get rid of them," he insisted. "Imagine you're taking all the junk and negativity and throwing it into the deep water. The sea's hungry, it gobbles up everything."

The young man's hands went to his chest and tears flowed down his cheeks as he made slow, rhythmical movements towards the water. He experienced the sensation of a heavy part of him being torn away as he imagined throwing his pain into the sea. He didn't ponder on the meaning of his experience. Whatever had happened, his discomfort had eased and he was calm. He turned towards the fisherman, touched him gently and mumbled his thanks.

"That's good. Now it's all gone. Let the fish worry," the fisherman said with a smile. As they talked heavy clouds formed. Suddenly huge swells rocked the boat and the young man, still seated on the edge of the boat, was tossed into the swirling water. His body writhed as he struggled to breathe. The fisherman threw him a rope but the young man turned his head away as he wrestled with himself. Though a large part of him wanted to slip down to the sea bed, an inner voice told him to take the hard way, to fight for his life and grab the rope. He made his decision and seized the rope. The fisherman hauled him out of the water. Heaving and spluttering the young man collapsed at the bottom of the boat and fell into exhausted sleep. On waking, he found that the storm had passed and the sky was clear.

They were eating sandwiches the fisherman had brought along, when the young man pointed. "Look over there, at the light over the water." A faint golden glow had spread across the sea, highlighting the ripples and a soft arc of light shone in the sky. An eerie stillness hung in the air. Neither of them spoke. As the light faded, the fisherman started up the engine and steered the boat back to the beach.

TWENTY-NINE
꧁꧂

DEPRESSION IN OLDER PEOPLE

The incidence of depression is far higher in older people than in the rest of the population. However, depression is not an accepted and normal part of ageing. It is a serious condition at any stage of life. Family or doctors may easily miss signs of depression in an older person and even confuse them with dementia. As older people are expected to be slower, to eat and sleep less than before, their symptoms of depression may be overlooked. As a result, an older person suffering from depression might be left untreated and continue to suffer unnecessarily until the condition worsens or becomes life threatening. It is well known that older people are frequently preoccupied with thoughts of death. If their thoughts turn to suicide, their symptoms must be taken seriously and immediate treatment must follow.

The Department of Health and Ageing in Australia estimates that due to the increasing ageing population, by 2012 the rate of major depressive disorders amongst the elderly in Australia is likely to reach approximately 14% of the general population.

Symptoms of depression to be aware of in older people:

- Sleep disturbances.
- Feelings of low self-worth.
- Extreme fatigue.
- Loss of interest in former hobbies and other pastimes.
- Social withdrawal.

- Neglecting personal care and hygiene.

- Slowed movements and speech.

- Weight loss or loss of appetite.

- Thoughts of death and suicide.

Age brings changes

Each person reacts and adapts differently to the changes age brings. While some older people welcome a time to be freer with less responsibility, spending time with children and grandchildren, others may feel overwhelmed and only see negatives.

- *Retirement* – Reduced income and an inability to enjoy former pleasures may result from retirement. After leaving a job held over many years, hours of unfilled time and boredom may be all that seems to lie ahead. Work that was once the source of a sense of value to society, independence and self-worth is now gone.

- *Illness and frailty* – An older person may suffer from increasing illness, frailty and pain. Former activities might be curtailed or even stopped and a loss of social contact might follow.

- *Loneliness and loss of independence* – For some older people having to live with children or even move into a retirement home can mean a tremendous upheaval and a loss of independence that implies the end of a useful life. The choice of living alone can be lonely.

- *Loss* – With advancing years loss is inevitable. Friends, relatives and possibly a spouse may die. This may be extremely hard to bear and grief may continue for longer than expected. Grief and depression share many symptoms and telling them apart is not straight forward. Though sadness, lethargy, tearfulness, decline in appetite and insomnia are all typical reactions to the loss of a loved one, within about six months to a year, the mood usually begins to lift and interest in life gradually returns. With depression, constant brooding tends to intensify. If thoughts turn to suicide, urgent treatment is necessary.

How to help a depressed parent, relative or friend.

- *Give unconditional support:* If an elderly person feels sad, lost and alone your unqualified love and support can help to relieve depression.

- *Find an understanding doctor:* A doctor and a team of health professionals with experience in working with older people, can both support your parent and provide up to date care.

- *Maintain your pattern and style of living:* Try to continue doing as many of the personal and family activities with your parent as possible by seeking extra help where necessary. In this way an older person will not feel they are a burden.

- *Try to be positive:* Accept that your parent may take some time to recover from depression. Expect that there will be days when your parent appears to have recovered and then he slips back again. As long as there is a move towards improvement, however slow, try to be optimistic. Do your best not to display your concern or any negativity to your parent.

If you feel unable to care for your depressed parent or relative

Face the issue and discuss it first with your partner or relatives. Then talk to your doctor about alternatives, such as placement of your parent in a retirement home or aged facility. Try to be objective about any decision made. If you have tried your best but cannot for whatever reason continue to care for your parent, do not allow yourself to feel guilty. Your guilt feeling might only make a relationship with your parent tense and difficult. Realise that caring for an aged parent is one of the most difficult tasks to attempt.

The difference between depression and dementia

Often dementia and depression are confused in an elderly person as many symptoms can overlap. Depression is present in dementia patients but depression does not automatically mean that a person has dementia. A thorough physical examination by a doctor can help to confirm a diagnosis. One of the important differences between depression and dementia is that antidepressant medication can alleviate depression, while drugs can only slow the decline of dementia.

These are some basic points to help you to identify dementia:

- *Memory*: While depressed people often have trouble concentrating and are forgetful at times, they remember what happened the day before or what they said a short while earlier. People with dementia have trouble remembering most things. They also may have trouble remembering how to bake a cake they baked all their lives or how to tie their shoe laces. The names of simple objects they use frequently are forgotten.

- *Orientation*: Depressed people know who they are, where they are, the time of day and so on, while people with dementia can be confused about all of these factors.

- *Fabrication:* A depressed person is usually concerned about memory problems while a person with early dementia may try to fabricate a story to cover the problem. When dementia sets in they are unlikely to be aware of their condition.

- *Loss of vocabulary*: A person with depression may not want to talk about their feelings but a person who has dementia may lack the vocabulary or ability to discuss how they feel.

Communication across the generations can be extremely difficult. Depression makes this even harder. Each generation has values and attitudes that differ but listening and sharing ideas is the best place to start.

Case study

Brian's father Arthur was 75 and a widower. His grief over the loss of his wife had continued relentlessly since her death three years earlier. He was tired all the time and complained of a lack of energy when previously he had felt young for his age and still active. He no longer drove to meet his friends at the bowling green or to play his weekly game of poker. After staying home week after week he lost contact with friends. As he no longer used his car he asked his son, Brian, to sell it.

He was now dependent on Brian and his wife Jenny. He didn't trust taxis and so his children drove him everywhere. Though grateful for their help, he viewed himself as a burden to them.

Brian and Jenny found life increasingly difficult. They had two young children and now dad to deal with. He was moody, often grumpy and tended to make sarcastic remarks about their child rearing methods, saying that his grandchildren were spoilt and could do with a "good hiding" to keep them in place. Brian developed resentment towards his father's remarks and had trouble sleeping. When he was honest with himself, he longed for his father to be in an aged facility or home.

Jenny managed to ignore her father-in-law most of the time and the children kept out of his way. She came from a large, caring family who looked after their elderly parents but they were nothing like Arthur. They helped in the home and were pleasant, even sweet tempered. Her mother had knitted Brian a sweater for Christmas and her father had made toys for the children from left over wood. She had not come across an old person as moody and difficult as her father-in-law. Worse still, he had refused to take the medication his doctor had prescribed.

At his next appointment, Arthur's doctor came straight to the point. He told Arthur that he was upsetting the family with his behaviour and demanded to know why he hadn't taken the tablets he had prescribed. He warned Arthur that he would find himself in an aged facility if he didn't take more responsibility for his life.

The appointment with the doctor gave Arthur a jolt. He decided to take his tablets and made an attempt to be more pleasant. After three weeks he noticed a change in himself. He was able to get out of bed in the morning without help and started taking short walks.

On a warm sunny day he phoned one of his old friends and arranged a game of bowls. Greg was so keen for him to join them again that he offered to give Arthur a lift to bowls twice a week and later arranged for someone else to pick him up for poker.

Arthur couldn't have been more pleased. And Brian and Jenny watched Arthur's progress with relief.

THIRTY

LIVING WITH A DEPRESSED PARTNER

Depression changes the structure of a relationship and the roles of each partner. Living with a family member or partner who is depressed can be demanding and at times distressing. It is natural to initially deny the symptoms and try to ignore them but depression is a real illness and a loved one can't "snap out of it" or just "pull his socks up" and feel better.

Prior to this depression you and your partner may have had an equal relationship, each having your say and each sharing the running of your home and caring for family. All this can change when a partner is no longer well enough to carry out a share in the housekeeping or take a former role in the family. Now as carer, you have a new role and possibly a more dominant one.

Some suggestions:

- *Learn as much as you can about depression:* Read as widely as you can on the subject. The more you know about it the easier it will be for you to cope and the more realistic your expectations will be.

- *Encourage your partner to seek help*: He will be most comfortable talking to a doctor he knows and visits regularly. It is likely that the doctor will refer him on to a mental health specialist. Though you can suggest your partner seeks help and encourage it, you cannot force the issue. Being positive and speaking confidently about the role of health professionals in the treatment of depression may help. Offering to make an appointment may help as long as your partner agrees to it. Even suggesting visiting a local doctor for a general medical check-up might be the start of seeking further help.

- *Don't try to rescue him from depression*: All you can do is offer support and unconditional love. You are too close to him to even attempt to solve his problems.

- *Maintain your routine:* Try to keep to planned appointments and meetings with friends and family members if possible. However you may have to cut back your work hours or involvement in studies, exercise or hobby courses in order to spend more time with your partner. This may mean that you see less of children or grandchildren and you will need to explain the situation to them.

- *Encourage physical activity:* Encouraging your partner to resume interest in sport, hobbies or interests that once gave him pleasure is a positive approach but try not to push or insist. Activity may help to lessen the length of the depression.

- *Join in an activity:* Walking together and later going to a movie or out for lunch may be a way to involve and motivate your partner in being more active and in taking more of an interest in the world around him.

- *Be open and share your feelings:* If you are angry or upset, instead of living with growing resentment, try to be gentle but honest about your feelings. Always be clear about what you intend to do, and about those things you do not want to or cannot tackle.

- *Do not ignore talk of suicide*: There is always the threat of suicide during a depressive illness. Never ignore suicidal talk or argue against it. It is likely to be a way of seeking help. In all instances seek help from your doctor or the nearest hospital, should you become increasingly concerned.

- *Talk to a counsellor or trusted friend:* Don't hesitate to seek support. You do not need to bear the pain of watching a loved one so ill alone. You are also likely to be tired, distressed and concerned about the future. Talking about how you feel to a trusted person always helps.

Intimacy and depression

Spend time being close physically and let your partner know that he is still loved and desirable. With increased fatigue and low energy levels comes a lower libido, so don't take your partners drop in sexual interest personally. Some anti-depressant medications have side-effects that may affect sex drive. It is best to discuss this with your doctor.

The most important thing is to remain close as a couple, to be intimate in discussion, in touching and sharing of thoughts and feelings. Expectations of slow improvement rather than an immediate return to full sexual activity will help you both ease into a return to a normal sex life once the depression lifts.

How to talk to your partner about depression

In the early stages, it can be difficult knowing what to say to a partner who is depressed. You might be afraid of saying the wrong thing or upsetting him further. If your partner has withdrawn, communication can be difficult and upsetting. Never take what is said personally. Realise that you are witnessing the depression manifesting itself. Listening and empathy is of key importance. Just being there in a non-judgemental and caring way is what is needed most. Loving encouragement and hope will be a key support and motivator.

Healing story: *Partners*

David and Marilyn sat on the drab couch, while outside a neon sign flashed. They were travelling to visit a sick relative in the country and had stopped at a motel for the night. As the television bleated senseless messages, she sat at one end of the couch and he at the other, their hands held tensely in their laps. They had barely spoken a few words to each other for weeks. If there wasn't a change, they knew that their eight year old marriage was doomed.

Through the thin wall they could hear each painful word of the row between a couple in the next door room. A choked voice pleaded, "tell me that you love me."

There was a cutting silence and then, "you won't leave me, will you,?" the woman begged, "please tell me you won't."

The man cleared his throat and the sound reverberated through the thin walls.

"Get rid of her, please."

"I don't know", the man hesitated. "I don't know...I need time...time to sort myself out. I do love you in my way," he muttered. "I just need my space".

There were sounds of sobbing and one of them blowing their nose.

"I've loved you so much and so well during these years together. Why...what made you do this? Betray my trust? "The woman thumped the wall as she spoke. "If you go back to her I'm leaving."

"Don't pile on the pressure, it's too much...I told you...I need my space." the man answered loudly.

David and Marilyn looked down, unable to face each other. Hearing their own situation played out in the next room shocked them both.

David's dark head was bent and his lip trembled as he recalled how idyllic their relationship had been when they were newly married. A surge of resentment rushed through him as he thought of her lack of interest and attention since the children were born. They had consumed all her time and affection. Guiltily he thought of Gina his secretary – attractive and good company and most of all she listened to him. Breaking up with her meant having to fire her. He hated confrontations but he knew that he would have to do something about her soon.

Tears flowed down Marilyn's face, as she recalled the difficult years she had stood by him in the business and done without so that he and the children could have the occasional treats. She wondered whether she could remain in the marriage even if he sacked his secretary. Turning her head away, she shielded her tears with her hand. She had put up with the long, lonely evenings waiting for him to come home far too long. Her earlier anger and hurt at discovering he had been with Gina was now a numbness. She sighed as she remembered how she had adored him when they first married.

After their second child Geoff was born, she suffered from postnatal depression. Of course there had been miserable times in her life, but nothing like this heavy, pervasive sadness that seemed to gnaw at her insides most days. It seemed strange that her depressed mood suddenly swung, to leave her elated for a day or so and then just as soon returned her to desperation. The instability of her mood frightened her and she doubted she would ever recover.

Her first birth had gone smoothly with only a day or two of "baby blues" until she felt fine again. With her second pregnancy, she didn't look forward to the pressures of caring for two small children with little money. When her lack of resentment towards the new baby grew her doctor recommended counselling and prescribed antidepressant medication.

Gradually her sadness and fears eased in severity. Even she thought it strange that instead of her earlier indifference, she began to love him fiercely. She became totally involved and protective of him, to the exclusion of her husband and everything else.

In the early morning, the biting cold hung between them as they resumed their journey in silence. Suddenly a truck swerved on the slippery road and hit their car. Both were thrown into a ditch. They were both unconscious for a short time after the accident and taken to hospital. In their shared room, Marilyn struggled to wake and kept slipping back to loving times years ago with David. They were hand in hand on the beach watching the sun rise over the water after a night of passion. The scene changed as they walked down the aisle on their wedding day, with smiles, white tulle and flowers. There he was, his face puckered with anxiety about their future, but holding her, gripping her hand as he glanced at her admiringly. She could feel him stroking her head as she gave birth to their first son. Loving images of David and the children flitted past her inner eyes. Loud voices interrupted her memories. She saw white coats and sniffed the antiseptic, hospital smell as she began to surface.

David remained unconscious for longer. He heard her sounds in the background but preferred to watch the pictures of the two of them making love on the rug in front of the fire, tenderly holding each other afterwards. Then she was in the kitchen baking a layered chocolate cake especially for him, his favourite since childhood. There she was, the perfect mum playing quietly with the two boys. The scene changed and he saw her in her business suit, cool and efficient, helping him to run the office. The images of them both and the children kept changing as he heard her voice calling his name. The past was comfortable, but her voice was insistent. When at last he opened his eyes, she was resting in the bed next to him.

Their hands moved beneath the white starched sheets and across the beds to touch each other reassuringly. It was the first time they had touched in weeks. They turned towards each other and wept at the thought of what might have happened. Weak and shocked they were reluctant to continue the journey right then and booked a hotel room. Relaxed on the sofa, they talked for hours. Before making any other promises, David insisted on sacking Gina as soon as they returned.

PART 8

SUICIDE

THIRTY-ONE

ADULT SUICIDE

Why people turn to suicide

Why does someone who appears to have everything to live for decide to take their own life?

Parents, relatives, friends, lovers and teachers of those who have attempted suicide are plagued by this question. For those of us who have never been on the verge of suicide, it is an incomprehensible, irrational act. The fight to survive at all costs, to hang onto the last breath of life is the norm, but when people become severely depressed, there is always a danger of suicide.

For a person who has reached a point of utter hopelessness, who sees no future, suicide appears to be an option. It may seem as if all choices have dried up and there's nowhere to turn to ease the anguish. By now, usual coping strategies have failed and life seems hopeless, empty and unbearable, and the future looks so bleak that each day is an insurmountable obstacle course. When one is no longer thinking rationally, suicide seems to be the only escape from interminable emotional pain. Some people contemplating suicide might think that the only punishment that suits his or her evil nature or "badness" is death-suicide.

Protecting yourself against suicide

As depression takes hold, suicidal thoughts often present themselves more powerfully and can dominate thinking. If you are having suicidal feelings or thoughts as you read this, realise that you are feeling overwhelmed with emotional distress and you can no longer cope. It does not mean that you are a bad or weak person. Each person's ability to withstand despair is different and the point where they feel no longer able to cope is different too.

You may find some relief by realising that this self-destructive urge stems from your depression. It strikes hardest when your despair is at its worst and all you want is some relief. Fortunately, these feelings are likely to lessen in intensity and frequency or even disappear with the appropriate medical treatment.

> *If you feel suicidal seek immediate help*! This is not the time for you to attempt to help yourself. Don't wait! You need professional help and you need it now. This book can only point you towards suitable assistance. At this stage, place yourself in the hands of someone you can trust and can speak with openly. Phone a friend or a help line listed on the internet or yellow pages.

Once the crisis has passed

These are a few measures to help you to protect yourself against future suicidal thoughts:

- Write a description of all the signs and symptoms of your depression at its worst. This way if you have any further suicidal thoughts, you will always be able to recognise your depression for what it is and you won't be influenced by it or become confused.

- While suicide is on your mind, get rid of medications you may be tempted to take and any objects you could use to harm yourself. If possible, ask someone reliable to help you by keeping your prescribed medication and giving you the necessary doses as you require them.

- List all the avenues of help available to you, with the contact numbers, in case you need them. Include several friends, relatives or people you know who understand your problem and who you can call for help at any time of the night or day. Phone numbers of your local doctor, psychiatrist, counsellor, several crisis lines and emergency at the nearest hospital should be written on your list as well. Make several copies of this list, place them around your home and keep a copy in your wallet. You'll feel safer knowing that they are there.

Case study

I'll never forget the day Angie told me about her son Jared's attempted suicide. Tears rolled down her face and she shuddered as she spoke:

"Jared was having a terrible time with depression, not eating or sleeping much and the medication the doctor put him on didn't seem to work. As you can imagine, he was pretty despondent about his treatment. One morning I overhead him say, 'I'm stuffed. I can't go on anymore. Maybe I should end it all.'

"I don't know how I could have been so stupid, but I was sure it would pass. All I could think of was to tell him to go back to the doctor, but he refused." She sighed before continuing. "It was Wednesday night, when I woke suddenly, and heard the sound of the garage door banging. The car engine was revving and immediately I thought of Jared. In a panic, I scrambled out of bed. 'Wake up, Eric,' I yelled to my husband. 'Hurry! I think Jared's in trouble in the garage.' I was outside in seconds and pulled up the garage door. The engine was chugging away and he was in the car. A plastic pipe connected to the exhaust pushed through a window was pumping in carbon monoxide. Eric wrenched the tube from the window, opened the door and turned off the ignition. Jared looked dazed but he was breathing. Eric helped to drag him out of the car and onto the lawn. I stayed with Jared while Eric dashed off to phone the ambulance.

"The paramedics were there in minutes. They raced him off to hospital. Believe me, I was relieved when a doctor told me that he was out of danger. We saw him the next day, looking frail and small in the white hospital bed. He cried when he saw us and we cried too and held onto each other tight. 'Sorry Mum, sorry Dad,' he whispered tearfully, over and over.

"I stroked his head like I used to do when he was a baby. Later that day he saw a psychiatrist, who decided that he needed to stay in the psychiatric unit for a few weeks so that they could sort out his medication and offer him some counselling. After that he started to improve.

"He's home now and going for walks and doing some mild exercise at the gym. He's hoping to return to work in a month or two, all going well. I relive the whole thing in my head day and night and I can't help feeling guilty. I should have taken more notice when he spoke about wanting to die. I didn't want to believe he'd do something like that and pushed it out of my mind. At least I could have talked to him about the way he was feeling.

"Perhaps if we talk more as a family and share our ideas and feelings, we may be able to help him if he hits a problem again. At least he won't feel so alone."

Learn about suicide

If those at risk of suicide are identified early and treated quickly many lives could be saved. If you understand more about the causes and types of depression that lead to suicide you may help save a life.

Statistics from the Center for Disease Control and Prevention in the U.S.A indicates that 38,364 suicide deaths were reported in 2010. This places suicide as the 10th leading cause of death in the U.S.A. The rate of suicide has been increasing since 2000 and was the highest rate of suicide in 15 years.

Though declining slightly, the statistics for suicide in Australia are still incredibly high. In 2008 there were 16 deaths per 100,000. The female rate was lower and remained at around five deaths per 100,000 since the late 1990s, dropping gradually from six per 100,000 females in 1997.

What to do if a friend or relative threatens suicide

A suicide threat from a loved one is frightening. Even the thought of such a tragedy is unbearable, but if someone close to you is severely depressed or suicidal, the best approach is to take some preventative measures.

- As it can be hard to determine how close to suicide a depressed person really is, never take threats of suicide lightly. They are definite cries for help from someone who is slipping over the edge. Although it may seem difficult, try to talk to the person threatening suicide.

- Feel your way, using your intuition and sensitivity, with gentle words. Hopefully, through discussion, the person thinking of suicide will be able to share and release some feelings of desperation and the suicide attempt may be averted.

- Always try to make the suicidal person feel wanted and loved. Gaining the suicidal person's trust makes the next step of insisting on seeking help far easier.

- Try to make a contract with the suicidal person, joining forces to counteract the suicidal feelings. The depressed person must promise not to make any attempts at self-injury without speaking to you or other nominated people first.

- It would be best to go a doctor or hospital with a suicidal person, but if this help is refused, phone a crisis line or the emergency number so that a trained person can come to your aid. This is the time to act. Never wait to see if the crisis will pass.

Suicide warning signs

Although intentions to commit suicide may not be obvious, some of these warning signs will help you to be more aware that a loved one may be at risk.

- Expressions of hopelessness and utter despair deserve attention, such as, *the future looks black, I can't see how anything good will ever happen. My life's hell on earth what's the point of it, I'm better off dead.*

- Giving away precious items to specific people, concluding business matters or spending time tidying personal papers, may be an indication of suicidal intent.

- Remarks about methods or plans of suicide, or about others who have committed suicide in the past should be carefully monitored.

- A person who has attempted suicide before should be watched carefully, as the same technique tried previously may be used again but with greater success this time.

- Watch for irrational behaviour. Some people are too depressed to think rationally. In a deluded state, they may believe that they have to kill themselves due to feelings of guilt or because they are being ordered to do so by voices in their heads.

- Watch for signs of increased use of alcohol or drugs. With any drinking or drug taking, judgment can become warped and reality distorted, making suicide appear to be a more attractive option than it would otherwise be.

- It seems strange that a depressed person is most likely to turn to suicide when vitality begins to return. With higher energy levels and keener organising ability, suicidal plans can be put into action. For this reason a person should not be encouraged to leave hospital too early or be considered depression free and out of danger, until mood stability has been established over many months.

To sum up, try to keep close to someone you love who is depressed and maintain communication at all costs, even if only a few words are exchanged. Never be afraid of calling for help. If you are wrong and there is no crisis, you will be relieved but one never can be certain, so it is best to take all the precautions available when threats of suicide are made.

Healing story: *Ground Zero*

On that fateful day in September, I was in an office, four blocks from the World Trade Centre, when I heard a booming explosion and felt a horrific jolt that rocked the first 110 story building. Horrified I stared out of the window and saw the top of the tower in flames. I was trying to grasp what I had just seen when an airplane hit the second tower. There is no way I can describe how I felt when both towers lit up and crumbled. I wanted to rush out and do something to help but I was paralysed with fear. Stuck. All I could see was the filthy cloud outside the window and the terrible images on the office television. How I eventually made my way through the smoke to the car park, blocks away and arrived home I don't know.

My partner drove me to a doctor after I hadn't eaten or slept for three days. He told me later that I had sat staring for hours. I was at home but I felt like a stranger there, unattached and uninvolved. The scene I'd witnessed played over and over. I smelled the smoke and saw and heard the screaming figures hurtling down to the ground. Accusingly my own voice yelled at me, *why them, why them and not you? The least you could have done is gone out and tried to help*. Each morning I woke with my face wet with tears. Later, the images changed to survivors covered head to toe in ashes, running, limping and being carried out by fireman and volunteers. In my dreams I saw shrines of passport photographs of couples celebrating their wedding, people smiling at office parties, at boat shows and in their gardens at home.

Gradually my dreams appeared less often but I was unable to work and just about managed to buy groceries and clean the house. I felt so shaky and the slightest thing upset me. One night I had a dream that I believe helped me to recover. I returned to the office to collect some papers and looked out of the window as I had when the attack occurred. Seeing the devastation of Ground Zero was a shock even though I'd seen it countless times on television. When I looked out again, I noticed tiny green shoots, the sharp green of new plant life, growing aggressively over the charred site of destruction. Their vibrant tentacles had crept up bent steel girders, lush grasses covered broken bricks and distorted concrete. Flowering bushes sprouted and mounds of white and yellow daisies flourished amongst the blackness. Trees had shot up swaying in the breeze and birds sang on their branches. In my dream it was transformed into a living, natural park – a magnificent memorial to those who were hurt and had died there. When I woke there were no tears on my cheeks. I dressed and went about my chores with more zest than usual. In the weeks that followed, I began to heal, to come alive.

THIRTY-TWO

TEENAGE SUICIDE

Teenage Suicide is growing at an alarming rate throughout the world, but it is preventable. Recognizing warning signs and learning how to respond to suicidal teenagers at risk can save lives. Most importantly never take warning signs lightly. Seek immediate assistance. The Australian Bureau of Statistics shows us that suicide is a leading cause of death among young people, second only to motor vehicle accidents. Suicide increases rapidly during the teenage years, between 15 to 19 years and then it increases again between 20 to 24 years. In rural areas the rate of male suicide is almost twice the rate of males who live in cities. The rate of suicide in indigenous communities is far higher than in non–indigenous groups.

Why teenagers are committing this tragic act

Growing up has always been difficult and adolescence is a period of rapid change in the bodies, minds and spirits of young people. It's a time of spiralling hormones and intense feelings. Many teenagers can be moody and withdrawn. Sensitive young people have extremely powerful emotional reactions to traumatic experiences. A broken romance, the shock of an unwanted pregnancy or the guilt of a termination, the hurt over a break-up in their parents' marriage or disappointment over a failure in end-of-year exams can be very distressing. Without the resources of adult experience and maturity, many teenagers feel unable to cope with intense emotional distress.

In spite of a typical adolescent's outward fight for independence, the support of family and friends is needed more than ever. Life at this age is filled with new and often devastating difficulties such as alienation from peers, lack of communication with parents and siblings, and feelings of being alone or unloved. All of these factors can severely disturb a young person's general emotional state. Feelings of anxiety and confusion about a future career or finding a suitable job can also make the future look hopeless for a young person. It's not surprising that at this time of turmoil many young people become severely depressed and even suicidal.

One can never underestimate the role of drugs and alcohol in a despairing young person. Many young people turn to alcohol or drugs to drown their misery only to find that they are left with the worries they tried to escape. Alcohol or drugs can trigger reactions which distort perceptions and cloud reality and judgment, bringing a desperate young person to suicide.

Case study

Jared's mother has already told her version of her son Jared's attempted suicide. Now Jared's sister Tess, gives her account. She had feared that her brother would attempt suicide for a long time, but he parents ignored her warnings.

"Hardly a day would pass without him throwing his arms in the air and saying, 'I can't hack it any more, it's all too much'. He was drinking a lot and had begun to withdraw, first from his friends, then from us, his family.

I'd hear him pacing around in his room muttering, 'All I want is to be bloody out of it and be at peace. No one cares anyway.' Of course I was worried but Mum and Dad had some weird idea that talking to him about it might encourage him, so they said nothing. When he gave his friends his CDs and me his prized watch that granddad had given him, I panicked. I knew it was a sign that he was getting closer to action. I'd been listening out for him at night, just in case. He knew I was watching him and waited until I was out of the house to make his attempt.

I'm angry that he did this, after he promised me he wouldn't. How can I trust him now? He's recovering and I'm pleased, but the thing worrying me most about him now is his obsession to return to work so soon. I reckon that if he has problems coping at work and gets stressed, he could become suicidal again. I can only hope he talks to his counsellor about it."

Some specific indicators of teenage suicide

If you suspect that your teenager is thinking of suicide, watch out for these indicators:

- Changes in eating and sleeping patterns.

- Inability to concentrate.

- An earlier failed attempt at suicide is an obvious risk. Another, more successful attempt could be made.

- Neglecting hygiene and personal appearance.

- Withdrawal from friends and family.

- A tendency to sit alone listening to sad music, drawing and writing poetry or stories about sorrow and death.

- Dangerous driving, dare-devil stunts and increased use of drugs and alcohol.

- Staying away from work or school.

- Withdrawing from usual sporting and other activities that were previously enjoyed.

- Giving away of treasured possessions.

- Creating of suicide notes.

Always remember that severe depression in a teenager is a warning sign and should never be dismissed. It is possible that all of these warning signs may not present in a teenager's behaviour. However, it is advisable to heed even one or two warning signs.

What to do if your teenager appears to be suicidal

Suicidal signs are usually indications of severe distress and often a desperate call for help. Many teenagers don't understand their misery and don't know how to deal with their feelings. They are seeking acknowledgment of their emotional pain and for someone to help them. You can try to ensure your teenager's safety in the following way:

- Hide all drugs, sharp knives, blades and firearms until the crisis passes.

- Try to talk to your teenager about your concerns, but if communication is difficult or impossible, and help is refused, seek out someone he or she can confide in – a friend, favourite relative, doctor, counsellor, sports coach, grandparent, priest or rabbi.

- You will also need someone to guide and support you in dealing with this stressful situation. Don't try to cope with it alone, confide in a trusted friend or relative.

- Above all, try to be calm and in control. Your child needs you more than ever before.

- Don't lecture, moralise or minimise your child's pain, instead reassure your teenager that the depression or suicidal feelings can be successfully treated.

- If your teen worries about what appear to you as minor issues, listen and reassure your child that these issues can be managed.

- Most of all, express your concern and love.

Treatment after a teenage suicide attempt

Once a teenager has been medically examined and psychologically evaluated the treating doctor or psychiatrist may then consider one or more of the following options:

- Medication.

- Individual therapy with a psychiatrist or counsellor.

- Family therapy.

- Couple therapy (If a boy or girlfriend is closely involved).

- A stay in hospital.

The most common reason for admitting a teenager to hospital after a suicide attempt is to ensure his safety while a thorough evaluation of his state of mind is made. Hospitalisation does not always follow automatically. Frequently the teenager concerned is fearful that his peers and teachers might learn about his attempt. However the decision to hospitalise usually depends on how serious the attempt was in terms of planning and organisation. Allowing the teenager to return home will depend to a large extent on the understanding, love and support of his family and his doctor.

If you believe your teenager is seriously at risk of a suicide attempt, don't wait, seek immediate help. Your nearest hospital emergency department is your first resource, but if your teenager refuses to go to the hospital, phone your doctor. If the doctor is unavailable, phone a crisis line and request aid at home. Telephone crisis lines are an excellent support while waiting for help.

THIRTY-THREE

RECOVERING FROM DEPRESSION

When you are feeling well again, the very last thing you want to think about is a possible relapse. However depression can return even when treated. The best approach is to acknowledge the possibility and plan ahead to ensure that you remain well. If you had injured your arm seriously in a tennis match and it seemed healed, would it be wise to enter a long gruelling tournament without rest breaks, if you noticed twinges of pain? You need to ask yourself a similar question about pushing yourself too hard when you have recently recovered from a bout of depression.

Most importantly, realise that you can recover from depression and recover well. However, recovery rates vary according to the type of depression from which you have been suffering. If you are getting over a mild bout of depression you will find that you will return to your former activities and routine fairly easily and quickly. If you are recovering from a serious and lengthy depression it may take a little longer to feel well, and it will require your patience and care.

Take your time, easing yourself back into former activities and responsibilities without expecting too much of yourself. Expect to recover gradually, using the suggestions and strategies offered in this book to help you to regain your confidence and strength.

The following brief summary of points in the book will help you to remain healthy and free of depression.

How to prevent a relapse

Stress

Stress is part of our lives and one cannot predict pressures, frustrations or difficulties that occur. However, you can protect yourself by recognizing the signs and symptoms of stress and taking steps to reduce its harmful effects. You will cope far better than you have in the past if you adopt the tools and strategies in this book that best suit you. Experiment with the various strategies suggested. If one doesn't suit your needs try another.

Ask for help

Never be afraid or ashamed to seek help if you need it. Doctors and other therapists are there to help you.

Knowledge and understanding

Learn as much as possible about depression and the signs of depression mentioned in this book such as destructive thinking, feelings of hopelessness, sleep disturbances and poor appetite.

Experiment

Don't be afraid to experiment with the various forms of therapy available in this book. They are there so that you can do that...and find the one that suits you.

Be aware of negative thinking

Be aware of destructiveness in your thinking – of negativity, hopelessness, shame, guilt and fear of the future. Your thinking is an important sign of your wellbeing.

Express your feelings

Find ways of expressing how you feel in ways that don't interfere with or hurt other people. Expressing the way you feel in a positive constructive way takes experimentation and some maturity.

Relaxation

Use suggestions in the book to help to keep you balanced and relaxed.

Medication

If your doctor has prescribed medication for several months after an initial recovery, as is usually the case, do not experiment with the dosage or stop taking it without discussing it with him first. If you are having side effects from the medication or feel unhappy with the way it makes you feel discuss this as well.

Counselling

If you have been receiving any form of counselling or support whether from a psychologist, social worker, doctor or psychiatrist, maintain these follow-up sessions. You may find joining a depression support group helpful. Early intervention is important and may prevent or even lessen the severity of a further depressive episode. Do not stop your follow up sessions abruptly, thinking you no longer need the support. Always discuss this important step first.

Monitoring

Monitor your moods and do not ignore serious slip backs into a depressive mode. Go to your doctor if you suspect a relapse. Become more aware of the positive and helpful activities and people in your life and include them more often.

Lifestyle

Following a healthy lifestyle is an essential element in your recovery. Pay attention to eating well and doing some exercise. The development of a positive sleep routine is an essential element of your recovery. Use the techniques suggested in the book to achieve the restful sleep you need. Relaxation and rest during the day is equally important so follow up that area and allow yourself the necessary time.

Activities and interests

Being active is important for your general health. Start with walks and if you would like to, increase the extent of your activity to gym work or sport. Consider involving yourself in an interest or hobby. Any outside interest whether it is reading, writing a journal, painting or craft work, will involve you and lessen your focus on yourself, improve your concentration and confidence in your ability.

Socialising

It is important to socialise again. You may connect with old friends or form new relationships in interest groups or learning situations. It is your choice whether you decide to tell others about your depression or not. It does take time to trust enough so as not to feel vulnerable. Spending too much time alone and isolating yourself may contribute to depressive thoughts, so try to leave your home often and spend time in company.

I hope that this book has given you information and strategies as well as the confidence and courage to listen to your intuition and learn from your insights. Embrace the help offered to you through reading about ways of thinking, being aware and living in the moment, medication, doctors, counsellors, and alternative therapy. Though support from friends and loved ones will help you to remain balanced and well, in the end you will heal yourself. You will make your life worthwhile again. You will find your own way and make your own choices, face your setbacks and battle to recover over what often may seem a long period of time. Be spurred on and encouraged to follow your desire for change and fight to get well. The only way is forward.

APPENDIX
꙲

INTERNET SITES OFFERING ONLINE INFORMATION AND HELP

Better Health Channel

Better Health Channel is an Australian site based in Victoria that provides health and medical information, fact sheets on health conditions, healthy living tips and questions & answers from health experts.
http://www.betterhealth.vic.gov.au/

beyondblue

beyondblue is a national, independent, not-for-profit organisation working to address issues associated with depression, anxiety and related substance misuse disorders in Australia.
http://www.beyondblue.org.au/index.aspx?

Black Dog Institute

An educational, research, clinical and community-oriented facility in NSW offering specialist expertise in mood disorders including depression and bipolar disorder.
http://www.blackdoginstitute.org.au/index.cfm

Headspace

A community based service for people aged 12 – 25 and their families. Headspace provides help for issues including health, education, work, mental health and drug & alcohol use.
http://www.headspace.org.au

SANE Australia

SANE conducts innovative programs and campaigns to improve the lives of people living with mental illness, their family and friends. It also operates a busy telephone helpline and website.
http://www.sane.org

INTERNATIONAL SUICIDE HELP LINES

UNITED KINDOM

Samaritans is a registered charity aimed at providing emotional support to anyone in distress or at risk of suicide throughout the United Kingdom.
http://www.samaritans.org/

Campaign Against Living Miserably is a registered charity based in England. It was launched in March 2006 as a campaign aimed at bringing the suicide rate down among men aged 15–35. **http://www.thecalmzone.net/**

UNITED STATES
The National Suicide Prevention Lifeline is a 24-hour, toll-free, confidential suicide prevention hotline available to anyone in suicidal crisis or emotional distress.
http://www.suicidepreventionlifeline.org/

Please Make A Note Of The Relevant Help Lines In Your Own Area.

BIBLIOGRAPHY

Beck A.T. *Cognitive Therapy and Emotional Disorders*, New American Library. 1980

Brown Jonathon D. *The Self.* New York: McGraw-Hill; 1998

Burns. D.D. F*eeling Good – The New Mood Therapy*, New American Library. 1976

Cabot. S, *Help for Depression and Anxiety*. WHAS. 2009

Costello. J. E., Erkanli, A. and Angold, A. (2006), Is there an epidemic of child or adolescent depression? *Journal of Child Psychology and Psychiatry*, 47: 1263–1271.

Cartwright R.D. *The Twenty-four Hour Mind: The Role of Sleep and Dreaming in Our Emotional Lives*, Oxford University Press. 2010

Cleghorn P. *The Secrets of Self-Esteem*, Element Books 1997.

Copeland M. E. *The Depression Workbook*, New Harbinger Publications. 1992

Davison, T. E., McCabe, M. P., Mellor, D., Ski, C., George, K., & Moore, K. (2007). The prevalence and recognition of depression among aged care residents with and without cognitive impairment. *Aging & Mental Health*, 11, 82-88.

DSM 4: *Diagnostic and Statistical Manual of Mental Disorder*, American Psychological Assoc. 2000.

Ellis. A. and Harper R., *A New Guide to Rational Living*. Wilshire Book Company. 1975

Emfield M.and Bakalar N. *Understanding Teenage Depression.* Out Book, USA 2001

Freeman A. *Depression in the Family,* The Harworth Press, 1986

Eyers K., Parker G., Brodaty H. *Managing Depression Growing Older.* Allen & Unwin 2012

Gillett. R. *Overcoming Depression,* Lothian. 1987

Kapur S., Miexzkowski T, Mann J.J., Antidepressant Medications And The Relative Risk Of Suicide Attempt And Suicide. *JAMA* 1992; 268(24):3441-5.

McKeon. P. *Coping with Depression and Elation.* Sheldon Press U.K. 1995

Mark Williams, John Teasdale, Zindel Segal and Jon-Kabat Zinn. *The Mindful Way Through Depression, Freeing Yourself from Chronic Unhappiness.* The Guiford Press, 2007.

Miklowitz D. J. *The Bipolar Disorder Survival Guide,* 2011.

Naylor B. T. *Depression in Children.* Nova Science Publishers, 2010

Pennebaker J.W.(1977) *Writing About Emotional Experiences as a Therapeutic process.* Psychological Science, 8, 162-166.

Quinn. B.P. *The Depression Sourcebook.* Lowell House 1995.

Seligman, M, *Helplessness.* Freeman. 1975.

Siegel R.D. *The Mindfulness Solution: Every Day Practices,* The Guilford Press, 2010

Smet P.A., Herbal remedies. *New England Journal of Medicine.* 2002;347(25):2046–2056.

Strohecker, *Natural Healing for Depression.* The Berkley Publishing Group. 1999.

World Health Organisation, *Treatment Protocol Project*. Australia 2000.

Yapko. M.D. *When Living Hurts*. Brunner Mazel. 1988

Zuess J. *The Wisdom of Depression*. New Leaf 1999

INDEX